PERSONALITIES

AN EXPLORATION INTO THE ORIGINS AND DEVELOPMENT OF EXISTENCE

Dictation from The Great White Brotherhood

Bob Sanders

DISCLAIMERS

This is a free eBook. You are encouraged to share it for free (in unmodified form) to whomever you wish. If you have paid for this eBook, you should request or seek an immediate refund.

The author has made every effort to ensure that the accuracy of the information within this book was correct at time of publication. The author does not assume and hereby disclaims any liability to any party for any loss, damage, or disruption caused by errors or omissions, whether such errors or omissions result from accident, negligence, or any other cause.

COPYRIGHT

This book was authored by Bob Sanders and dictated to him from The Great White Brotherhood by clairaudience, or as some people call "channelling". It is free for everyone to read and share unmodified for spiritual advancement. Please share this book unmodified with anyone and anywhere you can to help spread the messages it contains. For more information please visit the following internet sites:

https://www.thegreatwhitebrotherhood.org

https://www.thestairwaytofreedom.org

https://www.youtube.com/channel/UC2UDv0r4mtNPEWbve5YHDeg/

First edition – July 2019

Cover Artwork by Paul Saunders

Author – Bob Sanders

ISBN: 9781086051834
Imprint: Independently published

TABLE OF CONTENTS

FOREWORD 5
CHAPTER 1 6
CHAPTER 2 11
CHAPTER 3 20
CHAPTER 4 27
CHAPTER 5 36
CHAPTER 6 44
CHAPTER 7 52
CHAPTER 8 58
CHAPTER 9 65
CHAPTER 10 75
CHAPTER 11 84
CHAPTER 12 91
CHAPTER 13 99
CHAPTER 14 114
CHAPTER 15 127
CHAPTER 16 133
CHAPTER 17 141
CHAPTER 18 147
CHAPTER 19 151

FOREWORD

What more can we tell you?

You may have noticed that these books are getting more and more advanced, more and more difficult to understand and we are pushing the boundaries of knowledge far from anything previously known.

We need to be careful because, although, as we have said, existence is endless in its dimensions and there is so much more to talk about, it would be pointless in going too far from anything you could possibly understand.

We have studied the reactions people have had to the book about aliens and we have noticed, as we suspected, people are breaking into two camps.
There are those who are fascinated by the information, who devour the information with a hunger bordering on gourmandize and there are those who, for a number of reasons, are not able to relate to the information, and so, just turn away.

This presents us with a problem, because we have been tasked with providing you with as much information, in as short a time as possible, to help with Ascension. But we don't want to leave too many behind.
However, there is a growing difference between those able and willing to accept this information and those who find it too strange, too different from anything previously known and so cannot go on.
We freely admit that this information is so different from anything previously expounded by so-called experts, that it does take a stretch of the imagination.

Book 5 was about aliens and was difficult.
Book 6 is about DNA and many, indeed most of you, will find it a real stretch to comprehend, because it explains the range of influence DNA has in all life, all dimensions.

So, we are approaching the place where the ability to comprehend for even the most open-minded of you will not go.

But, as we have said, we have been instructed to make information available to all as quickly as possible, so we will introduce you to the subject of this book, which is about life as it really is.
Not physical, not imaginary, but yet another "behind the scenes" area, once again, largely unknown.

Thus, many of you will find this book even more difficult to understand and accept then the previous books.

CHAPTER 1

INTRODUCTION TO THE UNKNOWABLE

Already, there are vast numbers of people throughout the world that are convinced that all that exists is physicality and we must admit that we have been guilty in saying this.

We did it for a reason.

We had a number of aspects of what appears to be physicality to explain to you and so there was no point in telling you that nothing exists except imagination and curiosity and that they are aspects of God's mind.
There was no point in telling you that, although God exists, he is an invisible force living in a "nowhere" place.

But, having taken several books and many lessons to explain physicality, we gradually introduced to you the concept that, in fact, all that exists is imagination and curiosity.

Now we must admit that this was not the truth either because, if we return to our onion that we have so often mentioned, it appears physical, But, if we peel it back layer-by-layer, skin-by-skin, we arrive at nothing in the sense of no evidence of any life force.

But that implies that, although something might be invisible it still exists.

We stated that a number of things are invisible but exist: air, gravity, electricity and many other things.

But we want to take you further back - or forward, depending on how you look at life - and say that there exists life beyond that invisibility.

We are not talking at all about something that can be measured but not seen.
That there is a whole level of all life that has no means of being quantified.

Obviously, if something cannot be seen, measured, weighed or even estimated, if something is unquantifiable, logically, it should be impossible to describe or to talk about.

But talk about it we must.

So we have our age old problem of where to begin.

We have said that all good stories start at the beginning, go on to the end then finish. But we have also described life as a wheel, with no beginning and no end.

While this is true, it is not all the truth.

For instance, incarnation, as far as the average person is concerned, is a straight line: birth, growth, decline and death.

But, we explained in the story about a straight line in the mud made by a cartwheel that, behind that straight line was a circular wheel turning, transporting goods, through the energy of the horse and the ability of the cartier, that life is really a turning circle with no beginning and no end.

This second description of the turning wheel may exist in physicality but is, can and does exist in the astral planes.

So we have two aspects to life:
1. A straight line from one spot to another or the progress of time from the past to now and, eventually, into the future.
2. Also we have this apparent circle of life.

We would like to bring to your attention yet another aspect we have mentioned in the past and that is the "now" moment and the "place" concept.

We have suggested and explained that, in effect, life only consists of countless now moments and, equally, there is no space and only the "here" idea.

Whilst this is also truth, and we hope that you have followed our other teachings to understand what we are saying, there are always other ways of looking at life.
We have the somewhat unenviable task of explaining in simple language this next level.

We want to wipe the slate clean and go back to the time where nothing existed.

We hope that you can remember from our previous books that there was a time, long ago, where nothing at all existed: no planets, no space … absolutely nothing!

Yet, obviously, something must have existed to create all that now exists.

This is where we have a problem because, the simple truth is that when we said that nothing existed, we really meant … nothing!

Not even God.

We apologise to people who cannot imagine a life without God and we have been guilty of telling you that God has always existed. The good news today is that God does exist and his power is growing stronger by the day.

But there was a time - if we may mention time - when we can go so far back in time to this "nothing" time and say that, at that far distant moment, not even God existed.

There was absolutely nothing!

So, from that strange time we need to find out how everything that we see, all that came into existence in this incredibly complex subject called life, came about.

So this is where we need to step into the void and find out just what happened to bring life from nothingness to all we have now.

This, as you can possibly imagine is not going to be easy to explain as we must introduce to you concepts that have never been described before.

The Bible starts from the moment when God created the heavens and the Earth, implying that there was a time when nothing existed and that God, happily for us, decided to step in and create everything.

Even in other religious texts, they generally start with creation.

Scientists talk about the" Big Bang" and spend a fortune investigating where everything came from - although we have told you how everything was created in other books.

But no one seems to worry about what was going on before everything was created, before God came to be.

There have been a few that have speculated, but no one has really been able to get to the truth of the matter.

We also have a problem in that, no matter how far our records go back, and they go back to the time of the Big Bang, for obvious reasons there are no records available before creation.

So, how can we possibly describe existence when there was no existence?
Fortunately, the answer is simple.

It is possible to go back to the time before all that we see in all the dimensions came into being, including the creation of God - for God was created by the simple process of delving into another reality.

So we have rather tricked you, in a way, because we said that, at one time there was nothing at all and now we say that there was something; another reality!

So did we tell you a lie?

One could answer yes, but we do not deliberately lie.
Sometimes we alter truth somewhat to gently explain reality (existence), but we would never lie to you.
That is contrary to our code of honour.

One should never lie.
One should always tell the truth even if one does not tell all the truth or masks truth in allegorical stories as the Master Jesus did so often.

Therefore, we ask you always to bear with us and, whatever we say in the beginning to introduce you to strange topics, we will always, eventually, guide you to the actual truth, as far as you can understand.

One of the major problems we have is that no matter what we tell you, there are always other levels of truth behind and beyond what we say.
Therefore, we are in the difficult position of never being able to reveal the ultimate truth about life because it would be totally incomprehensible to anyone.

So all that we tell you is true in its time and true in the limit of what we are talking about but can never be the ultimate truth.
To be honest, life and existence never ends so there are levels of experience, levels of new life constantly being created so the story never ends, nor will it ever end.
So, no matter how hard we try to describe life to you, it is always only relevant to the slice of time that we select to study.
Even as we are studying one aspect, countless other aspects are constantly being created.

Life never stands still so there will never come a time that anyone would be able to say that he knows all there is to know.

But to return to the subject of this book.
We mentioned that we played a trick on you by saying that there was a time when nothing existed but then we mentioned that there was life elsewhere.

It was a trick in a way but it was also the truth.
It is true that there was a time when absolutely nothing existed.
It is also true that life as we know it was created as a unique object, totally different from any other life form(s) created elsewhere.

Now, this is where the subject of this book is going to get difficult because we want to take you into a completely different form of existence to anything you could imagine.

As you can imagine, this is not going to be easy to explain.

Already, to imagine a time when absolutely nothing exists is a real stretch of the imagination.

But, if we can do a sort of mind exercise.

Please try to imagine a time when there was nothing.

No planet Earth, no life forms, no planets anywhere, no suns, no galaxies, no space, no time, no God, no Archangels, no concept of anything at all. Just absolutely nothing.

Can you imagine that?

Now, imagine yourself as the sole survivor, perhaps in a one-man spaceship or something, able to wander about in this nothingness.

Obviously, it would be quite impossible to do this because if there is nothing, there is nowhere to be!

But please go along with us.

If you could travel through this nothingness, you would, eventually, be drawn to another sort of area where there was life.

The problem is that this form of life has little or no relevance to anything we might experience or even imagine.

This is the task that we have set ourselves. How to explain life - if one can call it life - in another area?

So we will end this chapter here and start to delve into the real subject of this book, although we warn you that it is not going to be easy to explain, nor will it be easy to comprehend.

In fact, we would need to take you into areas where words do not exist.

Now, in the Heavenly spheres, we have the advantage that when we explain this book to students, we can create what you would refer to as holographic images to help students visualise the unknowable.

But in your reality, we have only words and so we have thought long and hard about how to tackle this problem.
We will do our best, just using words, to describe this strange place to you.

CHAPTER 2

AT FIRST GLANCE

So, we are going to broach this difficult topic of how to describe the indescribable!

Perhaps, if we may we will start by saying what this subject is not.

We are all, both those in incarnation and us in the spiritual realms, used to the reality in which we find ourselves.

We remind you that all who are part of the Great White Brotherhood, and we are many, all had incarnations at one time.
Some of our elder members had incarnations so long ago that life as you now perceive it on Earth was greatly different but, nevertheless, they did have incarnations and those incarnations, as they have been described to us, have managed to educate us to realities scarcely imaginable to the more recent arrivals.
But incarnations they were.

So, it is not easy for anyone who has not studied the subject of this book, to visualise areas outside of either incarnation or the Heavenly areas.

Equally, no matter how far we travel back in time, right back to the moment when everything was first created - and that was a long time ago indeed - could anyone visualise this subject.

So, we wish you to try to comprehend that no intelligence in any area could visualise what we are going to try to explain to you.

However, this area does exist.
Indeed, there are countless such areas.

It is only too easy to wish that what we have so far described to you is all there is in creation, but, unfortunately, all that we have so far discussed is only a drop in the ocean of creation.
It is, indeed, endless and we wish you to be able to expand your mind and realise that physicality, the spiritual spheres and all the other areas of life we have described is far from the limit of creation.

Now, this is where we are going to upset some religious people.
We must mention God.

God exists, as we have explained, not as an old, white man sitting on a cloud sending Hellfire and Damnation to all who do not conform to a particular religion, but exists as a sort of concept.

...fficulty in accepting that.

...you to the concept that the God we have described - complete ... a subset of a greater, far more expanded version of God that ...re is life.

...d of our galaxy is not the totality of God. Not lesser, but part

...y form of reality that we could imagine. In other realities there is also a version of God that created - no doubt with the help from other trusted servants - that reality.

Then, if we were able to move on to yet another reality, there will be yet another version of God that would have created that reality. On and on.

So we wish you all to try to understand that no matter how different, how bizarre life anywhere else is, there is always a version of God that can be seen as the guiding hand behind it.

Such is the nature of the creative force we call God, that his outreach is truly endless.

However, the amazing thing about this God force is that, not only are there countless versions of God in all these different realities, but our studies have shown that there is a definite link between all these versions and it is our understanding that all these different versions of God are aware of what is going on in any other reality.

So, we are implying that the God in charge of the remotest, unlikeliest version of any reality, is aware of and in contact with the God that created "our" version of reality.

This is a strange concept to contemplate.

It is fairly easy to imagine that God is so far reaching that he might well have created alternative realities but it is harder to imagine that each reality has its own version of God remaining exclusively with each reality.

We seem to be putting a limit on God's power, suggesting that he can only deal with so much and so there has to be multiple Gods to deal with all the different realities, each one confined to that reality.

In a way we are, not because we think that prime creator has any limit, but for the reason that God is so intelligent, so powerful, that he deemed it wise to create different versions of himself in order that each version could, independently, create each version of existence.

But we also said that each version of God has links to all the other versions and so all these Gods, although able to act quite independently to each other, nevertheless, remain linked in permanent contact together, sharing wisdom and growing together.
Even God is not a static, all knowing entity.
Quite the contrary!
God is constantly evolving as life evolves.

God might well have created all life everywhere but he is not so arrogant as to be above learning from experience of the life he created.

All returns to him, wherever that life might be and these versions of God, independently and collectively, benefit from the individual experiences of these various life forms.
That information is shared to all the versions of God no matter how remote from each other they might be.

This information about multiple versions of God will be new to you and might be a bit confusing and alarming to many but it happens to be true and we have been charged with transmitting this truth to you.

We hope that it will help you realise just how wonderful this creative force is, that it was able to create multiple realities and create independent, but linked, versions of itself to oversee these different creations.

So, whether you can accept this or not, we are presenting to you, possibly for the first time, an expanded view of the creative force - God - which, we hope, should give you an even greater respect for God then you might already have.

Now, as we have explained in relation to our reality, God is the life force but does not actually involve himself with creation.
There are trusted Archangels, sometimes referred to as the Directors of Life (although these Directors of Life are not the only forces involved with creation), and there are also other Archangels that help create other aspects of our reality.

We break off here to explain how we were informed about these other realities which will be the subject of this book when we can get around actually to talk about it.

We do apologise for taking so long to start to explain alternative life but we hope that, in order to clear the decks, so to speak, we need to create the base from which we can try to make sense of this other reality - one of many.

There are, as we have mentioned, two types of Archangels.

There are the ones created to serve God in creation and there are those who are human, have passed the final test and have progressed almost to the point of being absorbed in the Godhead. And some of them do, but others remain to serve for long ages.

This last group, wise beyond any recognition, are so close to the Godhead that they have knowledge of these other areas.

They do not, as far as we are aware, actually visit these other areas, but they are aware of them through the link with "our" God who, we told you, has links to other versions of God.

So, thanks to that link and thanks to these incredibly wise and generous human Archangels, the information has been passed down to us lowly beings (compared to them) and so we are able to pass that information to you.

We hope you will be appreciative of just how generous these beings are in sharing their wisdom with us.

While we are talking about Archangels, may we mention just who the beings are that have charged us with revealing all this strange and new information to you.

We wish you to appreciate, just talking about our reality, that there are many levels in the heavenly spheres.

You may have heard people talking about Ascension as rising from dimension to dimension and of high beings located in ever higher dimensions.

This is not at all true.

We have described in great detail all of the eight dimensions and have stated that various aspects of life are contained in different dimensions, each aspect having links to the other dimensions, in part at least.

Now, rising in holiness has nothing to do with dimensions. The Ascension process has nothing to do with leaving one dimension and rising to another, neither physically nor spiritually.

You, at the moment, have your physicality based on the 6th dimension and the Higher Self and other parts of you are based in the 5th dimension, with links to all the other dimensions with the exception of what is referred to as the lower three.

In fact, outside of physicality (when explaining things to you), we never refer to any dimension by giving it a number.
We only do this to try to explain existence to you in a way understandable to you.
We think of the dimensions as one huge dimension rather as one might consider an octave of music, although it consists of individual notes, as a glissando of sound.

So, it simply is not true that, as any person rises in spirituality, he would change dimensions.

If you are incarnate and on the 6th dimension, no matter how holy you might become, you will still remain on the 6th dimension.

If in the Heavenly spheres, you will remain in the higher 4th until you merge with the Godhead.

However, spirituality causes people to be at different levels within those dimensions. This is not actually, literally true.

The very wise and noble beings, far above us, are invisible to us, not because they are in a different place to us but vibrate to a higher frequency than us.

If we can imagine the spectrum of light from total lack of light (blackness) to pure Starlight (blinding white light) you can imagine that there are many frequencies in between.

It is very similar with spiritual growth.

The person who has little spirituality would not glow very brightly whereas a very advanced being would shine with a brilliance approaching pure starlight.
Obviously, in between are many levels and there are humans (discarnate) in all these levels.

The beings that have asked us to instruct you in spirituality live in fairly high levels but are still very much in touch with both us and you.
As they are aware of the shift of the Pendulum, the biological clock of the Multiverse, they have asked us to try to bring you up to speed on the requisite information that, together with meditation etc., will enable those who so desire to ascend in spirituality.
But, we repeat..
You, as you grow more spiritual, would be seen by those with psychic vision as glowing more brightly as all your atoms change frequency within the dimension in which you currently live, but
you will not be going anywhere. You will not be changing dimensions.
However, you will be changing greatly from within.
You will become more loving, more peaceful, more understanding of those lesser than you.
You will be able to accept all life as it is and not look down - or up - to anyone, except God, of course.
You will radiate this fundamental aspect of God and of existence … love!

So, we have spent quite a lot of time hedging around the subject of this book and, to be honest, we could fill a complete volume with what this book is not about, but we will not presume upon your patience anymore but will try, gradually, to take you into this book which, as we said, is about life in a totally different area that is outside of anything mentioned in any book and outside of anything we might have described to you before.

We should really start a new chapter at this point, but as this chapter is short let us make a start in introducing it to you.

Now, the first thing we wish to say to you is that we want you to put behind you anything that you think you know about life.
We want you to try to dismiss from your mind anything you learnt at school, anything that life has taught you and anything that we have mentioned in the various books, videos and lessons that we have made available to you.

The only example we can give you is to imagine that you had spent your entire life just studying one subject, gardening for instance.
So, all you really know about is gardening and you might have become quite expert on that subject.
Then, suddenly, someone asked you to stop studying gardening and to start to study another subject; quantum mechanics for example.
This would come as a shock and would require you making quite a mental change.
Well, this, in a way, is what we are suggesting you do.
Forget all you know and start again.

So, let us start at the point where, in our little spaceship, we discover this strange new area.

You may remember us saying that our galaxy, if it could be observed, would actually resemble an enormous sphere, with a coating of gravity surrounding it to protect it from being bumped into by any other galaxy wondering about.

This galaxy, if we may describe it as a galaxy, looks nothing like that.
The best we can say is that it looks like an enormous mist floating in a void.
This is, of course, only an approximation because we have no means of describing this new place, so we must use words with which we are all familiar or we could make no progress with our explanation.
So, let us call it a mist.

What does it look like?
A mist is usually white although, of course, a mist, if it is of chemical origin, might be of any colour.
This mist we will also call white.

However, as we look at it from afar, we notice that it is not static.
It is as large as our galaxy is but, as we look at it, we see that it morphs into different shapes, almost as if it were sentient.
We will see, later, that it is sentient. It is alive. Every bit as alive as any creature on Earth is alive although its life force is not like life on Earth.

So, if we stop at a safe distance and regard this galaxy, we see it constantly changing shape. The only parallel we can use from Earth is to describe a shoal of fish that moves in a great band as the shoal moves, so if we observe it, we see it constantly changing in shape as it ambulates across an ocean.

This galaxy resembles that somewhat but, can we say that it is progressing through nothingness?
We cannot really confirm that because nothingness, by its very nature, implies lack of space so, although it changes shape, we have no means of measuring movement.

We suppose that, if we had any means of calculating progression, it might be moving but we cannot confirm.

All we can be sure of is that it changes shape, pulsating, growing larger and smaller with, occasionally, parts that stick out for a moment, only to withdraw and the galaxy sized mass of mist assumes other shapes.

Obviously, with such a large "object", this happens very slowly so we do not want you to imagine that it moves, expands and contracts quickly. It does not. It all happens very slowly.

Now, this is where, once again, we need to presume upon your credulity.

If you were to study this galaxy for the duration of your lifetime you would not notice much difference but as time is relative, it does change shape.

If we could film, for long ages, this mist and then play back the film at very high speed, we would see it as we described, pulsating, expanding and contracting and, possibly, advancing across the void of nothingness.

We break off here to say, just once, that what we will say about this object, for the duration of the book, has not, we think, been directly observed by anyone. Not even the human Archangels.
It is information gleaned by the most advanced human Archangels directly from the God Force, with whom some are in touch and we remind you that "our" God is in touch with all the other Gods in all these other life areas and so what the God of this alternative galaxy knows, our God knows, which is passed on to some human Archangels and is, in turn, eventually, passed to us.

So, what we will describe to you is obtained by this means.
That will avoid us having to repeat, endlessly, the source of the information.

Whatever we say about this area has been collected by the means we just described.
Of course, you may accept or reject this information.

So, to return to this galaxy sized mist, it moves rather like an amoeba, constantly changing and we question whether it is alive?

Now, we could say that our galaxy is alive - and it is - but it does not seem to move as a composite whole whereas this one does.
We could say, equally, that a shoal of fish is not actually alive although it is created from countless small fish who are alive and their collective movement gives the shoal the appearance of life.

So we need to ask if this mist is alive in its own right or is it created from tiny objects, themselves alive, and giving this mist the appearance of life through the individual and collective movement.

We will examine more closely this huge mist and try to determine what is going on.
For the moment, we observe the mist and see it undulating, pulsating, swelling and reducing.

Suddenly, we noticed that it withdraws to a point, a sort of singularity, stays like that for a while and then, just as suddenly, expands to something like its former shape and continues its slow perambulations.

What on Earth is going on?

Then, just as suddenly, it expands to truly enormous size, sort of convulates on itself, almost as if it were turning inside out, reduces to a singularity and then expands to its former galaxy sized shape and continues as if nothing had happened.

We need to explain this as best we can.
The only example we have in our existence is a sun that, when it comes to the end of its life, expands dramatically, and then contracts to a very small area.

What we are trying to explain is not quite like that but gives us a basis for understanding.

So, let us explain again in slightly more detail.

This galaxy sized mist spends a while pulsating gently as it wanders about and then, without warning, it might contract to a single small point.
We use the word singularity because that is as close a word that we have to what is occurring.

So, every particle of this mist - assuming it is made of discrete particles rather like the large number of fish in a shoal - suddenly, and instantly, contracts to a tiny point.

We might ask if this point contains the life energies of the individual parts from which it consisted and whether this point has enormous mass (weight).
But, in nothingness, these terms might well be meaningless.

So, it stays as a point for a while and then, just as suddenly and just as rapidly, expands to something like its former size and continues as if nothing had happened.

Then, later, it seems to do pretty much the opposite.

It will suddenly, and without warning, seem to explode.

It grows to enormous size and, just at the point that we think that the individual particles that go to make up this cloud my surely wizz off into the nothingness, it seems, from the outer edge, to fold up on itself.
The outer edge seems to meet at the middle, all the rest follows until it is all absorbed, once again, in this point, this singularity.
And it stays like this for awhile.

The only example that we can think of to explain this in simple terms is to consider a pastry chef who might take a ball of dough, spread it out, and then take the outer edges and fold them into the middle.

Not a very good simile, we agree, but if you can visualise this enormous sphere suddenly expanding to an unbelievable size and then, just as suddenly, not withdrawing in the opposite sense to how it expanded, but folding up on itself so that the outer edge of this truly enormous sphere is drawn into a tiny point, followed by all the rest.

How can we possibly describe the reality of that stupendous event?
We just ask you to imagine if you will the outer edge hurtling into the centre, followed by all the rest until only a point remains.
Then, after a while, it expands to its former size and continues its route as if nothing strange had occurred.

Now, we must say that what we described above is true in principle but the reality defies description.
It is slightly different from our description but, as we said, words do not exist to describe any of this so we have described this mist using words with which you are familiar.

If you could be there to observe this mist and its Shenanigans, you would agree that the way we described it is correct but the reality, if you could observe it, would be much stranger.

However, if we must describe this entity, we must use terms and images with which you are familiar.

Actually observing this place will need to wait until we reach God like status and, even then, we may only be informed about it in the third party fashion.

But, we repeat. This place is real and what we have presented is as close as we can get using words to describe what occurs.

So let us stop this chapter here and take a closer look in the next chapter.

CHAPTER 3

THE BIG SQUEEZE

We have examined this strange and rather alarming mist but curiosity drives us to investigate further.

The only way we can really do this is to approach it and try to see, from a closer vantage point, what is going on.
But we need to be careful because, if this galaxy decides to expand or, indeed, to contract whilst we are in contact with it, we might be engulfed in its movements.

So, with some trepidation, we approach.
What we observe is somewhat startling and difficult to accept.

We wish you to accept that, as we reach towards this galaxy, it reaches out to us. Or rather an aspect of it does. We see a sort of projection, almost like an arm, reaching out to us and surrounding us.
Thus, we are engulfed in a part of this mist.

We wish you to visualize that the majority of the galaxy remains a fairly long way away but a part of it seems to have sensed our interest in it and has reached out to make contact with us.
So, we find our little spaceship surrounded by this mist.

It doesn't seem to want to harm us. Indeed, the feeling we get is almost of a welcome, a friendship. We get the impression that this mist is exploring us to find out who we are. Perhaps we are the first strangers who have ever made contact with this galaxy and it is curious to know who we are, where we come from and if we are friend or foe.
The arm of this mist withdraws, taking us with it and we are drawn into the body of the galaxy.

So, we find ourselves inserted into this mist and, much as we suspected, although from a vast distance it looked like a mist, once we are within it we find that each - what looked like drops of water from a distance - are, in fact, a vast number of orbs of life.

Now, we cannot effectively describe these life forms so we must use words with which you are familiar in order to convey what we are observing.
So, we will say that we are within a countless number of spheres of living objects. These spheres, although identical to our eyes and our senses, we realize, contain life in an individual and collective sense.
By this, we mean that each sphere clearly has a sense of being individual, like all humans are, for instance, but at the same time has a sense of being one.
The only example we could possibly use is to mention a huge ocean which, although created from individual drops of water, nevertheless reacts as one entity. An ocean

appears to react as a complete body, the individual drops of water no longer retaining any sense of individuality.
Once again, it is difficult to explain what we are observing.
We ask you to imagine, if you can, being inside this galaxy sized object, each element of it clearly created of spheres that have a sense of individuality but, collectively, moving as one object as if the whole object had an overriding intelligence.

Of course, we have similar things on Earth.
A person, for instance, is made from countless atoms which, we ask you to imagine, have a sense of individuality, of intelligence, but collectively create a person who is able to move as a composite whole.
The big difference is that we sense that every sphere in this object appears to be completely sentient in its own right but also has the ability to act together with all the other spheres as a composite whole.

This is rather strange to us.

We can sense that every sphere, being alive as you and we are, and clearly curious to explore us is, in another sense, acting as a unit.
We imagine that, whilst those spheres that are close to us are observing us, the whole object is still pulsating and moving rather like an amoeba.

We do not feel the least threat, the least hostility. In fact, the overriding sensation we feel is a curious but warm welcome as if the spheres are glad we have visited them and are welcoming us into their midst.

For a long time these spheres observe us from a respectful distance, each sphere that is close enough to be able to see us obviously rather excited to know more about us and we, in turn, try to send out thoughts that we come in peace and wish them no harm.

We repeat that, in earthly terms, what is happening is doing so very slowly but as we are astral beings and thus immortal, time has no meaning to us.
A day or a thousand years of Earth time is one to us. Time is meaningless.
So, we are able to observe what is going on very much at the same level as this galaxy reacts.

These spheres, whether they can pick up our thoughts or not are obviously not frightened of us.
It may be that fear is unknown to them.

Certainly, they seem excited that we have visited them and are curious to make acquaintance with us in order to understand us.

Gradually, one or two come closer to us until they are almost touching our little spaceship.
We can feel their presence very strongly.

Once again, how can we describe their emotions that we sense, as words - or, indeed, our emotions - because we do not have any connection to their emotions?

Certainly, if we try to present to you what we feel using familiar words we sense curiosity, friendliness, respect and even a form of love or should we say, acceptance.

Obviously, these words can only be an approximation to the emotions they project to us because, as we said, there are no words to describe emotions totally different from anything with which we are familiar.

But we, in turn, attempt to reply using our emotions in the hopes that they can interpret and understand that we return their friendliness and mean them no harm and that we just wish to understand who and what they are.

It may seem strange to people reading this that we are trying to communicate with spheres of energy and sending them human emotions but, if one considers that we do this with animals that we call pets or, indeed, plants and these animals or plants are perfectly able to understand the love, respect and even admiration that we send them and they, in turn, are able to accept and respond to our emotions, perhaps it is not so strange that these spheres can also respond to us.

If they are alive - and to us they appear alive - it is not surprising that they have emotions and can accept the emotions we send them.
Indeed, it comes as a relief to us to note that they do have emotions, totally at variance to ours but, nevertheless, are sending love to us in their fashion.
After all, as we said, when we project love to an animal or a plant, it responds and sends us the love as they understand it to be. They send it to us in the form that they are able to generate, which might well be very different from our understanding of love but love is a universal emotion and so we are able to appreciate that emotion.
It is the same in this case. We sense that their understanding of love is very different from our interpretation but sense that they are sending us love nevertheless.

Once again, those who have close relationships to animals or plants are able to send human love to them and they can accept it as love and they send us their version of love and we can accept that.

Most emotions are universal: love, hate, fear or lack of fear, and any other emotion is universal and is able to transcend species without difficulty.

It is the same, or similar, in regard to these spheres of energy that are obviously sentient and are able to project love, acceptance and fearlessness to us.

This, then, raises a number of questions.
If these strange spheres in this strange life form that somewhat resembles a giant amoeba are alive, is the whole amoeba shaped galaxy alive?

Is it one body like an amoeba or does it more resembles a shoal of fish, the individuals being alive but the resulting shape caused by a huge number of individual, living fish not actually being a life form but just the result of a huge number of fish moving with one intent?

Obviously, we will have some difficulty in resolving these questions as we do not seem to have any means of having a direct conversation with these spheres, and as we doubt that we can find a means of direct communication.

However, as we have tried to convey to you, we are able to confirm some basic communication through the emotions of love, friendliness etc.
But our real interest is to try to understand who and what these spheres are and as much as we are able to comprehend about them. Equally, if they are interested in learning about us, we are willing to tell them as much as we can about us.
The problem, of course, remains that we need to find a common ground for exchange of information.

A long time passes during which a stalemate exists before, suddenly, this galaxy sized object starts to reduce in size.

We had previously observed this event and knew that it was going to reduce to a singularity. This, obviously, was a cause of alarm to us as we were somewhat concerned that, as we were trapped within the object, we would be crushed as the galaxy reduced to a single point.
The problem was that we could do nothing about it except to go along with the event.

We observed the galaxy folding up on itself, the outside folding into the middle until our turn came and we found ourselves being crushed into the centre.

Much to our surprise and relief, once inside this point of life - the singularity- we found that we seemed to remain much as we were before.
This was strange and is difficult to describe. From a physical point of view, if observed from the exterior, we might have seemed to be squashed with all the spheres into one single point but, from our perspective, nothing seems to have changed.
We are still as we were and the spheres remain as they were.

This is an event that we had never experienced before and caused much cogitation to try to understand how one can appear to be reduced to a singularity but, inside the singularity, life seems to be unchanged.

So we are experiencing something unprecedented in our knowledge, which at least leads us to admit that there is always something from which we can learn and from which we can expand our knowledge base.

However, it remains - or did at that moment - an experience that we could not resolve.
We also realised that, if this was happening, it must be based on factual experience and

thus must have a reason that should be capable of understanding if and when we had all the facts.

But for the moment, at that time, we just had to accept the reality in which we found ourselves and could only wait and see what would happen next.

The fact that we are here describing the experience indicates that this strange experience was resolved in a peaceful manner and that we survived to recount the tale.

So, let us proceed and state what we managed, eventually, to comprehend.

Once we arrived at this singularity and once all of the countless spheres of life had all arrived at the singularity, something even stranger occurred.

We heard - or rather we felt - a voice communicating with us in a telepathic manner. This voice communicated some information to us.

We were aware of this voice and we assume that the voice was heard by every sphere in the galaxy and we were all given the same message.

Basically, the message was this.

The voice that spoke was from the controlling force that, apparently, spoke to the spheres on each occasion that the galaxy sized sphere reduced to a singularity. It took the opportunity to impart wisdom in order to guide the individual spheres as time moved on. On the occasion that we experienced, information was given concerning the progress that the spheres needed to hear that would allow them to progress as a total unit and not as separate, individual spheres.
It urged the spheres to forget their individuality and to think and act as one unit.
It describes how this controlling force saw the future and, when every sphere could combine and act as one, then that galaxy could move outwards and join forces with other galaxies, eventually hoping and expecting that all the other galaxies in this vast universe would work together as one.
If and when this occurred, a level of harmony would be reached that would enable the controlling forces of all the galaxies to become one and that would allow a level of peace, love and harmony ensue in a manner never before achieved.

The message continued in a similar vein for some time.

We who were listening to this speech found it somewhat surprising and not a little confusing.
Of course, we agreed with the message but were surprised that this voice that spoke with such conviction could come from some, apparently, external force.
Our major concern was to discover who and what this force was.
We have no president in our galaxy.

We have wise and respected people who give us similar information but those people are humans who have lived for long ages in the Heavenly spheres. This voice seemed to come from nowhere but caused no surprise to the spheres listening to the message as they seemed to have experienced similar events each time the galaxy compressed to a singularity.

The problem we faced was that we could not actually communicate with any of the spheres and thus we could not ask who the voice was because it was obvious that the voice was coming from an intelligent source and thus the voice was coming from a living force.

The next question we wanted to ask was where are the other galaxies to which the voice referred?
Did the voice refer to our galaxy or did it refer to galaxies as yet unknown to us?

It was obvious that we needed advice to assist us to comprehend what was going on.

Therefore, we did what we have done before. We seek help from the very wise human Archangels as we have done before.
For those who do not know what we are talking about, we will explain.

We have stated that there are many galaxies and each one has a God force in charge of creating each galaxy, or rather, creating the life forces and creating the Archangels who, in turn, create all that exists in any galaxy.

We have also stated that each God force, despite acting independently from any other God force, acts in a way such that each and every God force understands what all the God forces are doing. They share their knowledge.

But the very advanced human Archangels are so close to our God that they know as much as our God does.
As our God force knows what all the God forces know, so it is possible for our archangels to know what the God force of the galaxy we are questioning knows.

We are able to question our advanced archangels and they have been kind enough to tell us what they know.

This is what they told us.

First, there are countless galaxies, each galaxy exploring an aspect of emotion: love, hate, beauty, ugliness, kindness and it's opposite, growth, decline and so forth.

This galaxy - or rather its God - chose to explore peace as its theme.

Second, we might think that peace would equate to love, but it is not so.
Our God explores love but it is possible to live in peace without love.

Beings can live in peace together without sharing love. Peace can be a cold, sterile emotion whereas love has to be a sharing concept. It is not possible to love in isolation. Love is a sharing concept with all things but as little as two people can live together in peace.

Third, the archangels went on to state that the voice giving the message of peace was a collective result of coming together as a singularity.

This is difficult to explain in simple terms but we can say that, as the spheres come together as one, so that oneness enabled the motivating energy of the galaxy to express its basic nature; peace.

So the voice was coming from the very nature of the creative force. Not from the God force of this galaxy, nor from any archangels involved with its creation but from the prime creative concept of the galaxy.

This is a difficult concept to understand but it is important to accept that the theme of a galaxy is waiting patiently to express itself and, in this case, the coming together as a singularity provided the conditions for that prime force to express itself.

If we can accept that, it provides that our galaxy, if it can all join together as one, our prime creative force could and will be able to express our galaxy's Modus Operandi; love.

We repeat that we do not refer to God when we mention this. We refer to the fact that the galaxy, like all galaxies, is a living, thinking object, has a brain, emotions and everything any person has - all is one. Therefore, as a person can express a point of view, so a galaxy can express a point of view.
But, in order to express a point of view it needs to have every aspect of life in our galaxy coming together to be receptive to the message.

The prime motivation of our galaxy is love whereas the motivating force of the galaxy we are studying is peace.

Perhaps that is why, when we discovered this galaxy, there was no fear, no aggressivity but curiosity and friendship.

So we remained patiently within this singularity until it decided to expand to its former size again and, as we have described before, it carried on its perambulations as if nothing had happened.

CHAPTER 4

A SINGULARITY: A POINT IN SPACE TIME

Let us continue with this strange tale of a galaxy far from us that behaves nothing like ours and yet, as all life is one no matter where it is found, there must be a connection between our galaxy and this one.
We have to try to realise that, in some way, the manner in which this galaxy performs must have a link to ours but, for the moment, that connection seems vague indeed.
We can, at the moment that we describe in this tale, find absolutely no connection between the life forms that constitute this galaxy and ours, so we progress as we can and hope that a connection will manifest itself eventually.

We used words like 'story' and 'tale', which are usually words used when describing made up yarns, but we wish you to accept, if you can, that the events we describe in this book are true.
It may all read, so far, like a created tale but what we are trying to describe is an aspect of life, of creation, that is true but just seems so remote from anything with which we are familiar that it seems made up.
We could say that it is made up, but not by us. We report what is known about this galaxy and hope that you can accept that it is the truth.
Everything is created and so the creative forces that worked together to produce this strange galaxy tasked themselves to create an area in which the God force overseeing it all was able to explore the theme of peace.

So, having said that, let us return to the point that we left off in chapter 3, which was within a singularity listening to the motivating force of this galaxy expressing the desire for all of it to come together in peace.

Eventually, of course, we know that the galaxy expanded again but before we follow that event let us talk about a few things relative to this galaxy.

We mentioned that the whole galaxy reduced to a singularity but that all of us, both us in our imaginary little spaceship and the orbs themselves were all reduced to virtually nothing but were in no way harmed.

This, surely, needs some explanation as it seems to be a contradiction.
Scientists often imagine that, in the case of a black hole for example, once reduced to a singularity, life would be extinguished but our experience shows that this is not so.
Life in a singularity continues.

Therefore, we must assume that singularities have been incorrectly described.
Let us try to analyse just what a singularity is.

We know that this will take us away from our main story which is describing the galaxy we contacted but it will be appropriate and useful if people can understand what a singularity is, its purpose and how life can continue once inside one.

We imagine that a singularity is a tiny dot of "something".
This is both true and not true. Or should we say, as is often the case, it is true but not all the truth.

To fully examine a singularity would require a book in its own right so we hope you will forgive us if we just outline the concept and leave a complete description for another time.

To understand what a singularity is, we need to examine, somewhat, matter.
Once again, to fully explain what matter is would require a long treatise.
We are getting, once more, in to deep water because matter seems to exist but, in fact, does not.
Matter is illusion, part of the great illusion of physical life.

We have attempted, in other works, to suggest that matter does not really exist and all that exists is consciousness and imagination which together, give us the ability to imagine that matter exists.

But from our perspective, matter does seem to exist. Indeed, it seems to be the prime creation of our galaxy and also other galaxies.

We can hardly think that, as we look around us and see all that exists, that it is all an illusion.
If we bang our head against a brick wall, it hurts!
This can hardly be imaginary pain and we forgive anyone who rejects the concept that matter is illusion. The truth is sometimes stranger than fiction and the plain and simple truth is that we create matter with our imaginations.
So powerful is imagination, so powerful is illusion that matter seems real: people, animals, plants, planets and so on.

So, if you, we, can accept that matter is illusion and that nothing physical actually exists, why do we imagine it to be real?
Is there a point that does exist?
Can we locate something that we can say is physical?

Once again, the answer is both yes and no.!
We must repeat that nothing physical actually exists but there is something that we call consciousness.
So, what is consciousness?
It is a force that exists in a way connected to life and yet is, in another way, not connected to life.

You may remember in chapter three us stating that the prime directing force of the galaxy we were contacting talking to us.
That force is consciousness.

How can we describe consciousness in any meaningful manner?

If we take a living onion we may be able to realise that it has a form of consciousness. It is possibly self-aware. It is alive and thus has the desire to grow and to reproduce and we might call all that desire its consciousness.

And yet, if we peel the onion, layer-by-layer, we find no life force. There is nothing associated with the many petals that we could identify as its life force, it's awareness that it was alive before we killed it by peeling it or chopping it up.

So, this consciousness is an invisible force that exists but we can never make contact with it.

If we consider all that seems to exist, all the people, animals, plants, earth (Including rocks, stones, sand), air, water and so on, the one thing that we can say is that it is all alive and is conscious.
And yet, we said that physicality was an illusion.
So, if nothing exists actually and yet many things seem to have a life force attached to them that enables them - people, animals, plants - to develop, that force we suggest is consciousness.

Therefore, if we could see life as it really is, the only thing that would exist is the individual consciousness of everything that seems to exist and all of this is connected to the consciousness of our galaxy.
We put it to you that, if anything at all exists, it is the conscience of the galaxy and we further suggest that this consciousness of the galaxy is the singularity that we originally attempted to describe.

We repeat. A singularity is the consciousness of our galaxy.

This, of course, applies to all galaxies. Each galaxy has its own conscience and thus its own singularity.

This may seem somewhat confusing and difficult to understand so we will elaborate somewhat in an attempt to clarify and make it more apparent just what a singularity is.

We imagine that matter, in all its diversity, exists but, as we said, it is an illusion.
Matter does not really exist.
It exists in the individual and collective consciousness as a concept, an imaginary form that enables us and everything else to have the appearance of form.
This is necessary because without the idea of matter, life would have no basis in which to be able to have experiences.

Those experiences are what enables us to proceed in maturity both material and spiritual.

It is the struggle with apparent reality that enables us to mature as life forms.

As we have said, and we repeat once more, matter does not really exist.
However, if we take matter away, what we are left with is nothing.
Not just empty space but absolutely nothing!

So, if nothing exists it would, logically, be impossible for any life form to manifest itself because even spiritual - non-physical - requires a spiritual form of matter in order to exist.

The reality is that there is nothing in any dimension that we could call physical because physicality in any dimension requires a form of matter in which to manifest itself.

But life does exist and, in the absence of any form of physicality, can only exist as a non-physical energy we call consciousness.
However, as we have also explained before, there is only one form of consciousness.

This also is difficult to comprehend.

If we consider all the people who have lived in the past, are living now or will live in the future that makes a lot of people.
If we consider all the animals who have followed the same path, the plants, water, the various molecules (oxygen, hydrogen, helium etc.) the vast number of planets that constitute just our galaxy.
All that, collectively, creates a vast number of points of life.
And yet we say that any physical manifestation of these life forms are just illusions and that all that really exists is one point of consciousness we call a singularity and, from that one point of consciousness, all the illusion of all that we see and that history records is manufactured to enable life to appear physical.

So we hope that you can begin to comprehend just how difficult it is to explain this subject.

It takes a real stretch of the imagination to realise that you - if we may use you as an example - do not actually exist as a physical person and that you are just part of collective consciousness pretending to have a body, personality with strengths and weaknesses, living in a world that seems so real and enables you to have countless experiences each and every day but that it is all a form of illusion.

We do understand those who turn away and reject this concept. We will not try to convince you.

We have been guilty of saying, in the past, that life had physicality but that was because we knew that most of you were not ready for the information we now give you which, we

repeat, is that you, both you as an individual and you, collectively, as part of all life, only exist as part and total of this singularity of consciousness.
All that exists is an invisible point of life that we call a singularity and that is actually the totality of all life in our reality.

This point of reality - this singularity - may well be invisible but it is real and is alive. It is part of the only thing alive.
So, let us make sure that you have understood by looking at the subject in an opposite way.

There exists in our galaxy just one life form and this life form we call a singularity.

But the singularity has marvelous attributes. It can create the illusion that our galaxy is real and made up of a sun and countless planets.
Further, the singularity has the ability to create the concept of countless people, plants, animals, air, water and everything else that we see. It creates the illusion of matter.
Further still, with the help of certain archangels it can create the idea that we have thoughts, ambitions, hopes and aspirations.
It can create all the dimensions and heaven and hell.
In short, all that we have been talking about in the various books and lessons that we have given you is all created, one way or another, from this singularity.

But this singularity, being all that exists, is not only alive, but is a thinking entity, albeit, totally invisible to us or to you but can actually communicate with us all.

We had an example of this in the case we gave of an alternative galaxy reducing to a singularity which gave the overriding force of that galaxy the opportunity to convey information to the orbs in that galaxy and, by the same occasion, us who were trapped in the singularity.

We could go on to say a lot more about singularities but it suffices, for the moment, to understand that each and every galaxy in this vast enterprise created by the various Gods, to know that each galaxy is actually reduced to a single force that we call a singularity and so, just as there are an infinite number of galaxies, so there are an equally infinite number of singularities.

We will, perhaps, just repeat for the sake of clarity that all that actually exists in any galaxy is this infinitely small but intelligent life force that is termed a singularity.

Now, we are sure that there are many reading this that are confused because we have mentioned that each galaxy has its own version of God and those individual Gods create archangels to create all the illusion that any galaxy is made from.

So, if we may, we will try to explain the connection between any God, any archangels and the singularity from which everything stems.
We should also mention and explain where a Nirmanakaya fits in as well.

So, we appear to have a number of elements fighting and contradicting life.

Let us, for the sake of clarity, name just some of these entities and then try to explain how they all fit into the pattern of life.
We have mentioned, first of all, that there are a huge number of galaxies, each one existing separate from, but connected to, any other.
Within any galaxy there is at least one sun plus a large number of planets.
In our galaxy we have planet Earth and that planet is home to physical life.
Other galaxies may well have life forms associated with them but they are not life forms as we would recognise or understand them.
Then each galaxy has a God attached to it and that God explores an aspect of life (emotion) such as love, hate, peace, war and so on.
After that we find Archangelic beings -Directors of Life - that actually create all that any God desires to be produced.
We also mentioned Nirmanakaya.
Lastly, as far as this discussion is concerned, we have the singularity which has enormous importance in dealing with life.

If we regard the subject in a different order all that actually exists in any dimension - including what we call physicality - is the singularity that we have been discussing.
We could call this singularity the basis of all life.

Next, we have God.
Now, this is difficult to explain and to comprehend because most people consider that God is the creational force that is the start of everything. But we are suggesting that a singularity is the first thing that exists and God comes after.

So, who created the singularity?

We have mentioned that no one knows the origin of God but we know that we can link God to the singularity.
It would, perhaps, be impolite and incorrect to say that the singularity created God because we have the greatest respect for God even though we do not know the origin of God.
In a similar way, we do not know the origin of our galaxy's singularity.

We understand that, if the singularity did not exist, God would not exist but we, in truth, cannot say which came first - God or the singularity.
It is similar to the question or which came first, the chicken or the egg?
The chicken comes from an egg but without the chicken, eggs could not exist.

We have an identical problem concerning God and the singularity.
It is generally accepted that God is the force that creates everything but we do know that without the singularity, nothing would exist including God.

So, we must just accept that the singularity and God are closely combined just like the chicken and the egg and so, instead of endlessly debating which came first, the singularity or God, let us just accept that we need them both although we do know for certain that God and the singularity are two separate things.

Now, as we have just stated, there are a large number of "things" that appear real and without which life as we assume it to be, both physical and non-physical, could not be. We have filled a number of books which we have given you in discussing elements of life - physical, non-physical and spiritual - that require that these things seem real. But we have gone to some lengths also to tell you that none of it is factual in a solid sense and that all that exists, including God and his angelic forces, are part of the singularity which is also consciousness.

Now, assuming that what we have said is true, and if we did not know beyond doubt that it is true we would not have stated it, it implies that consciousness is at the origin of everything and all that follows on in any domain is created by consciousness.
It begs the question as to what consciousness is and where are its origins?
Is there an overriding entity somewhere; above and beyond God, that is creating in its mind all that exists?
Is this wonderful mind what we call consciousness?

We in the spirit realms have pondered this question for a great deal of time.
We have questioned human archangels who, we remind you, are so advanced that they are almost the equal to God and we have yet to receive a definitive answer.

We know for sure that the singularity is all that exists and this singularity incorporates consciousness.
We further know that consciousness exist in two parts: individual consciousness as applied individually to all things and collective consciousness as applied to groups.
We also understand that consciousness is constantly developing as life develops.
This, of course implies that there is a feedback system.

Consciousness creates all that we believe exists and it is all life's reaction to the experiences within the illusions that are fed back to the consciousness and the consciousness grows in wisdom very much as we have implied that God grows in wisdom through life's experiences.

Therefore, we assume that God and the singularity are very similar, very close, although we have been informed by the very advanced human archangels that the singularity and God are separate entities.

We are fast approaching the point where our knowledge concerning a singularity stops so, unfortunately, we cannot say much more on the subject. We dislike mysteries but there comes a moment, a point, where knowledge fails.
We will continue to investigate, to study and enquire as to the nature of singularities and, no doubt, at some point in the future we will become wise enough to comprehend this

mystery but, at the moment, we have to admit that we cannot provide you with an answer.

So let us return to us being inside a singularity.

As we look around us, strangely enough, we do not feel we have been squeezed into an infinitesimal point at all.
We are aware that this event called a singularity has occurred but, from our point of view, space looks very similar to what it did before we were all reduced to a singularity.
We assume that space is relative and, no matter what point one observes it from, space remains the same. So, what we are saying is that, from what we know about space and time, it is all illusion and, thus, if one is in space/time as we assume it to be in our ordinary world or whether we are reduced to a singularity, life, being all that exists, must go on.
We could not exist if we were squashed to nothingness and thus the illusion that we have living space (space in which to live) is produced just as it would in our normal existence.

We know from our investigations about life that all that really exists is a singularity, so we must assume that a tiny dot of space/ time is all that exists. So being inside the singularity is our natural state.

This, obviously, seems unreal because in a normal reality we can look around us and see lots of space. We can look into the night sky and see for millions of miles into space, but our infinitely wise human archangels inform us that it is illusion and that, in reality, we are all inside a singularity.

We remind you that a singularity is a dot of space/ time so small that it virtually doesn't exist, except as a concept. The singularity is so small that it could never be accurately measured by any measuring instruments. It could only be described in rather meaningless mathematical terms.
Yet everything physical, everything non-physical is contained in this virtually non-existent spot of space/time.
We apologise for hammering this point but understanding what an incredible object - if we can say that it really exists - a singularity is, is important.
It is fascinating as a mind exercise to imagine all of eternity in terms, not only of space but of time also (space and time being connected) contained in a spot of "something" so small that it can hardly be imagined, let alone measured, but once inside it space/time seems perfectly normal.

This, of course, is because, as we have said, our reality is contained within a singularity and we accept space/time as being real and endless in its dimensions and diversity.

Just as suddenly as this galaxy reduced in size, it expands again back to its former dimension and continues its perambulation through the nothingness in which it lives.

We wish that we could continue our instructions about singularities because we have not mentioned all that we know but this book is about this strange world we have discovered so we will end this chapter here, although we have not talked about this galaxy much but attempted to describe a singularity.

I hope you found this both interesting and informative as singularities are of paramount importance in life.
We will, in the next chapter, return to our recently discovered galaxy and continue investigating it.

CHAPTER 5

FROM MIND TO MATTER

We feel the galaxy starting to expand again. Just how long it took to expand from a singularity to a full galaxy again, we cannot say, as time is relative.
To us inside the galaxy it seemed like a very short time but we cannot truly say, in Earth time, how long it took and, to be honest, is of no importance. What is important is that the galaxy did expand and the reason that this is important is because, as we went to some length in the last chapter to explain, the singularity is all that exists and so we realised that this expanded version of the galaxy was returning us back to illusion once more. Or at least we reasoned that we were entering illusion again.
We knew enough about illusion to understand that this galaxy, just like ours, required illusion in order for it to have life experiences, experiences that it could not appreciate if trapped permanently inside a singularity, a single dot of consciousness.

Now, the thing is that in our galaxy, just on planet Earth, there are a myriad of life forms in all of the dimensions and that requires this expanded form of illusion in order to create what appears to be reality for all the life forms in all the dimensions and in all the abstract aspects of life: thought, desire, emotion, etc.

But what puzzled us was that the orbs that surrounded us all seem to be identical and none of them seemed to have any physical form different from any other, nor any sort of identity. The only attribute we could ascribe to them was that of peace as they reflected the motivating force of the God of that galaxy.

This seems illogical to us. What was the point of creating a vast number of orbs, clearly all alive, but with no distinct separate identities as far as we could see?

So, we thought about this and wondered if it was possible that the galaxy was more advanced spiritually and had outgrown independent personalities - ego based - and had progressed to the point where they reflected the will of their God?

This seemed a possibility but, itself, raised other questions.
If all the orbs had reached this stage and were now identical, what was the point of that?

Then we remembered that the voice that spoke to the orbs encouraged them to come together and reflect the will of their God - peace - so that implied that the orbs had not yet reached that advanced stage.

So, we hope that you can see that we had a dilemma, a mystery to solve.

On one hand, the orbs seemed identical and on the other we realised that the orbs had not reached the stage of being identical and of just reflecting the will of their God.

We felt the need to resolve this mystery or we would never understand what was occurring in this galaxy and, also, common sense told us that there must be a connection between them in their galaxy and us in ours and, if we could find out what was going on in their galaxy, it might have a bearing on how our galaxy might develop, assuming of course, that this galaxy was more advanced than ours.

It also crossed our minds to wonder if the opposite obtained and that this galaxy was so primitive that the orbs had not yet developed independent personalities.

In any case, we felt we needed to try to find out just what stage of development this galaxy was at and as much about these orbs as possible.

The huge problem was, of course, as we have previously mentioned, we seemed not to have any means of communicating with these orbs as they did not seem to have any language or, at least, any language with which we were familiar.

We were all well versed in telepathy but even this did not seem to provoke a response that we could identify with.

We managed to find an answer to this problem eventually and, if we may, we will explain, although it might seem improbable or even a bit foolhardy.

We decided to see if we could enter one of these spheres and connect with them that way.

So, we sent out a thought that we would like to do this and, much to our surprise, one of the spheres came up to our little spaceship and enveloped it.

We should, at this point, admit that we were not actually in a spaceship. We were in a sort of globe of consciousness, protected by a form of gravity.

We mentioned a spaceship in order to keep our description of travelling through nothingness and of entering the galaxy simple, but now, in order to keep the story going in a comprehensive and understandable manner, we must admit that it was in a sphere of consciousness.

However, in reality, one of these orbs blended with us and accepted us into their world.

It was most strange and a feeling that none of us had experienced, nor one that we could imagine.

We will attempt to explain although, as is often the case, we are limited by words and words do not always exist to convey sensations unknown to Earth humans but we will do our best to convey our impressions.

As a means of opening this explanation, may we suggest what one person might experience if he were to blend with another person. We refer to humans and human experiences.

We are all separate in the sense that we all have feelings, sentiments, emotions and ideas that are unique to us as individuals, although, as we are all connected and as there are only a limited range of these feelings we would, if we as humans blended with another human, expect to experience feelings that we would be familiar with.

We would expect to find love, hate, peace, anger, fear, calm, family attractions, feelings of sexual attraction - or the opposite - and so on.
The range is relatively limited so whatever we would be aware of in terms of emotions within ourselves, we would expect to find in other people.

Of course, some feelings might be more prominent in one person than another but most people have a range of feelings, of emotions present and we can all share those feelings.

But how do we explain or even, ourselves, understand feelings and emotions totally at variance to any with which we are familiar and how could we expect these spheres to understand the feelings and emotions we have which would be at total variance to them?

However, we have two points of reference. The first is that we know that the prime directive of their God Force is peace. This is a feeling with which we are familiar and that we share with them and, second, they accepted us into their world and thus we must share acceptance with each other and also feelings/emotions like trust, confidence and the common desire to share experiences.
So, we do share some feelings. This is a start!

We should, perhaps, explain the process of sharing feelings and emotions and how it works.

We do not physically blend or mold with one of these orbs.
We link our minds and do our best to put our feelings and emotions on hold and allow the orb with whom we are linking to direct his feelings and emotions to us.
Thus, we replace our thoughts by the orb's and, effectively, become one with the orb.

At the same time, we sense that the orb does much the same and thus can link with our minds.

So that is another thing that we have in common - the ability to exchange thoughts, feelings and emotions.
As you can imagine, this is a fairly advanced form of spiritual exercise and not one that could occur between primitive entities.

We should also point out that such actions do not imply a highly developed degree of holiness.
There are, in our realities, creatures, beings, entities that are decidedly unholy: black magicians, Archons and some aliens, that have developed the ability to stifle someone's thoughts and replace them with their own.
So, the ability to share thoughts does not automatically imply holiness. But we feel we can trust these orbs and allowing them to probe our minds, would not be negative.
We will also point out that we, ourselves, are sufficiently developed as to be able to reject any advances by these orbs if we felt any malign intentions.

So, we are doing a 'mind link', if we may thus express the process and allowing the orb that we are in contact with to probe our minds. We must be fair to the orb in question and if it is kind enough to allow us to explore its feelings and emotions, we feel that we must reciprocate by allowing it to explore our feelings and emotions.

We mentioned that we already knew we had a few things in common but when we really linked with this orb, we reached a stumbling block in that there was virtually nothing to which we could relate. But we battled on to see what we could discover.

The first problem we found was that the orb was not constructed of any material with which we were familiar. We are sure that most of you are aware of what is called the periodic table and the various elements; oxygen, hydrogen, helium, etc., and are also aware that most, if not all, matter is made by combining these elements in various ways to construct metals, plastics, glass and all the things we see on Earth.
Even bodies, human, animal, plants, rocks and earth are formed by elements found in the periodic table coming together to form everything.

But this orb and, by extension we imagine all the orbs, were created from elements unknown to us.
These elements remained unknown to us as we have no means of analysing just what their periodic table contains, assuming they have a periodic table.

Physically, they appear to be made from some sort of translucent material, the degree of transparency altering from time to time, presumably in response to changing thoughts or emotions. By which we mean that sometimes the orbs seem virtually transparent and sometimes quite opaque.
Why this should be, is a mystery.

Another thing we noticed is that these orbs are not fixed in their shape.
You will be aware that the majority of objects found on Earth tend to have a fixed shape, with the exception of some primitive life forms like amoeba or some jellyfish that can alter their shape somewhat.
The basic shape of these orbs is a sphere but, we notice, can alter to become elongated or pear-shaped, etc.
We also noticed that we never saw any of them becoming square or rectangular, triangular or pyramid shaped. Whatever shape these objects moved into was always based on spheres. Rather as if a sphere could be pulled into elongated versions rather like a rugby ball. There were never any sharp corners.

So, we were confronted with entities made of unknown material, able to morph into different shapes without there being any obvious intelligence causing this change of form and able to alter their degree of transparency, once again, without apparent reason.

What they thought of us is not really relevant to this discussion but we imagine that they were just as confused by our appearance and thoughts as we were by theirs.

Please remember that, as we said, we were in a sort of bubble, a sphere of consciousness protected externally by a coating of gravity. However, we were real entities within that bubble, not in physical form, but as spheres, also, of consciousness, each one of us with his own particular thoughts, ideas and emotions.

The exact number of us in the sphere of consciousness is not important. We mention it due to the fact that, if the intelligence in the orb we were investigating was singular, it may have been confusing to it to be picking up thoughts and feelings from multiple minds but that is not our fault. We travelled to this galaxy collectively and so were multiple minds.

To go back to the orb. What could we see when we entered it?

First of all, we could sense no life at all. We expected this orb to be a shell, a container for some life force but, although the interior was not totally empty, we could not feel that there was any living being inside it.

When we said that the interior was not empty but contained something, what we noticed was that it was full of a transparent sort of jelly.

We had experienced this before when we visited a place that had embryo lifeforms developing and we describe this jelly-like substance in a previous book.

So, this was something else we knew about.

We could not tell what the outside shell of the orb was constructed from because it was material new to us, but at least the jelly - plasma, if you wish - we had seen before, albeit in an area of life only distantly connected to our reality.

So, we repeat, we could find no life force within the orb. This pushed us to consider the possibility of the orb being alive in a global sense, in that the outer shell and the interior together created the life force because we were sure that the orb was alive.

Now, we could go on describing the long period of time that we cogitated this life force to no avail but, to cut a long story short, we once again contacted the human Archangels, who informed us that the whole galaxy, collectively, constituted its life.

Let us explain this in terms more readily understandable.

It seems that this galaxy was constructed of a large number of these orbs.

Each orb, individually, not really being alive but, collectively, the whole galaxy constituted what we might term, life.

It was only because of the total number of orbs constituting the galaxy that the galaxy of orbs became alive.

This is bizarre but not as bizarre as one might imagine.

So, if we may, we will break off the discussion of the orb under question and discuss the very important topic of life being connected to a coming together of disparate elements.

We have talked about this before but we wish to describe it again because it is one of the fundamental building blocks of what we call life and that life could not be if there were not all the disparate elements - humans, animals, plants and everything else, the physical and non-physical, existing that constitutes the conditions for life existing, at least in our galaxy.

Once again, this seems ridiculous but happens to be the truth, so let us expand on the concept in an attempt to make it understandable by all.

This is a very difficult concept to describe.
If you have read the information we gave you in at least one of our books, we mentioned that, in the beginning, God created a huge but finite number of points of life. A number sufficient to cover the needs of creation from the beginning until the demise of this galaxy.
These points of life are sufficient to cover all sentient life plus all the planets, etc., from day one until the end of time as far as our galaxy is concerned.

This is a ridiculously huge number of points of life, and could not possibly be imagined or calculated by anyone.
But the exact number of points of life were decided by God in conjunction with his Archangels and that exact number of points of life were created and placed in one of the dimensions. That exact number, no more, no less.
This does read like imagination gone wild but it is the truth.
Now, the strange part is that all these points of life are indestructible and will live forever, until, one by one, the points of life reach perfection and return to the Godhead.

Even stranger is the fact that, to create life, all of these points of life need to be there in order to create that life.
Whatever the number of these points of life are, and the number is beyond anyone's ability to calculate, that exact number has to exist in order for there to be life.
If it would be possible to remove even one point of life from the huge number, life would cease to exist.
If it were possible to remove just one point of life, the whole galaxy, including all the dimensions and all the life in the whole multiverse would vanish in an instant and there would just be nothing.
Not a vacuum. Nothing at all.
Fortunately, it is not possible for any point of life to disappear, so life continues.

So, what happens, in effect, is that this huge number of points of life - themselves not initially alive - collectively create life as we know it.
Now, we called the points of life by that name and, perhaps, gave the impression that they were already alive.
This is not quite true.
What we should have said is that they were potential points of life because it was not until they were all together in the 8th dimension that the magic happened and they all spring to life.

Life came into being in the form of all these countless points of potential life and, even more, if you can understand, those life forms created one life.
So, we have individual life in the idea of these individual points of life but also, collectively, these points of life came together and created one life form we call God.

We could use the example of a person who is made from a myriad of atoms, each one alive, but when they come together, they form a living person.
All, or most of the atoms that constitute a person, are necessary but it is the coming together of all these atoms that create a single, living person.

It is the same concept with a galaxy, universe, multiverse (call it what you will).
It is the coming together of all these individual points of potential life that creates them to be alive, both as individual points of life and collectively as one life.

We hope that you have understood what we were explaining.
Life can only exist as a concept, a potential, until every aspect of that life form, whatever it is; human, animal, plant or planet is complete.
Then, in conjunction with God's Archangels who control life by putting a logos with it, it springs to life as a single life force.
However, within that single life force, each disparate element also has a form of life.
We have explained this before by stating that every aspect of life is alive in an individual sense but, collectively, form a single life force we call God.

You may have picked up what appears to be a contradiction in what we have said.

We stated that God, in conjunction with his trusted Archangels, created the individual points of potential life but, once they were all together, sprung to life and formed one life essence that we called God.

This, at first, must seem bizarre to have individual points of life, only potentially alive, until all the parts are in place and then, and only then, does everything spring to life and form a collective and individual life.
But we have a similar event when a mammal is created.
At first, as it grows in the womb of its mother, the individual atoms - if we may use that word to describe individual life parts - gradually come together to form whatever the baby mammal is.
Each atom is potentially alive but remains connected to the mother by the umbilical cord which provides the substance to feed the atoms.
It is only at the moment of birth that all comes together and the baby mammal is born.
So, it is alive as an individual but each atom is also alive as can be demonstrated by taking a sample and growing it in vitro as is done with cloning animals. And so the process continues.

Let us return to the galaxy we were interacting with.
We gained the impression from the studies we quoted above that each sphere (orb) was part of the galaxy and so each sphere was a separate but essential part of this galaxy

which existed as a solo entity but relied on each and every sphere to be there in order for it to exist.
So, we have to assume that the sphere with which we were connecting was alive as it was part of a living galaxy. but we could detect no life force within the sphere.
So, in a way we were not much further forward.

On planet Earth, each atom of a living entity is itself alive as we just mentioned but, in this galaxy, there did not seem to be any life in the individual sphere we were studying.
But we were fairly sure from the way the galaxy behaved that it was alive.
How could this be?

The answer will take us on into an unknown form of life creation.

We could say that life is endless and, once created, an object, no matter how large or small it might be, has to remain alive for all eternity, ignoring its eventual disappearance into the Godhead far, far into the future.
But those who have followed our various talks or lessons will be aware that we have said that life is created, destroyed and created once more, countless billions of times a second.
So, our life in our galaxy does not exist eternally.
It is created and destroyed, created and destroyed, so we can hardly say that life in our reality is endless.
It is in a way, but as it is being created and destroyed, it is slightly altered due to the DNA of all things being adjusted and so, effectively, each time life is remade, it is a different life, slightly altered - from a DNA point of view - to the life that was destroyed a moment before.

It is the fact that the changes happen so fast that gives the illusion of one continuous flow of life.
In reality it is a series of jumps - created, destroyed, slightly altered as it is created again, then destroyed and recreated, slightly altered from the previous life.

If we could see life slowed down, we would clearly see that each frame, each moment of time is not only separate from each other but different as the DNA of all things is altered.
So, we would observe, slowed down, life as a series of frames, each frame slightly altered in its DNA to the previous frame.

What has this got to do with the strange world we are trying to explain?

We will attempt to explain this in the next chapter.

CHAPTER 6

THE SOLO LIFE FORCE

As the galaxy slowly expands to something like its former size, so we expand with it.
This implies expansion in two fashions.
First, we expand from a tiny dot, part of the singularity, to the size we were as we traversed emptiness on route for this galaxy and, second, we expand in the sense of moving away from the dot of the singularity and move out to space in the galaxy as does all the orbs.

This is impressive to watch.
The singularity expands and the orbs expand and form their previous shapes and, at the same time, the whole galaxy of orbs expands and assumes a space in the galaxy.

Eventually, the galaxy is expanded to the size required and seems to stop expanding but does continue to move slowly through what we might call space although, as we have said, there is not any space to move in.

So we watch as it continues to meander in rather an amoeba fashion as we have previously stated.

But we have learnt some things, the most important being that the galaxy is alive and it is the fact of each and every orb, independently and collectively, coming together that creates the galaxy being alive.
Further, the galaxy is one life.
We are familiar with this concept so it is a further link to the way life exists in our galaxy. So we realise that this galaxy is not so very different from ours. But there is a big difference in that the orb we are studying is only alive as part of the collective of orbs forming the galaxy and that none of the orbs appear to have any independent life of its own.

This is very different from our galaxy which, it is true, collectively forms life but, at the same time, the individual life forms have an independent form of life - an awareness - of consciousness.
Without that independent form of consciousness, nothing would exist. Not you, not us, not anything.

This, obviously, is a vast difference from our galaxy of which planet Earth, at least, is brimming with life of all kinds.

Now, we know that the galaxy we are considering is alive and the God Force animating it has peace as its prime directive.
We are also aware that this galaxy operates under different rules in that it is only alive due to the fact that all the orbs, collectively, create its life.

This pushes us to want to know more about the orb we are studying because we find it difficult to accept that the orb as an individual has no life force but, collectively, creates life.
Can you see the conundrum?
Each orb appears to be lifeless but when the orbs join as one, life is created!

So, we decide to investigate further the orb in the hopes of discovering how it can be both lifeless and yet contribute to life when acting in conjunction with the other apparently lifeless orbs.

We wonder if we can discover this secret it will open a door to another aspect of life apparently unknown to us.
As we have said, the orb in question has an outer shell made of some unknown material - unknown to us that is - and all that appears to be in the interior is a form of jelly, a plasma, and that is all.
There is nothing that seems to ask to be in any way connected to life and yet there must be.

We have often stated that there are no miracles.
No magic.
All is science, physics, no matter how impossible some things might seem to be.

If we could quote and example. There are some extremely skilled magicians able to perform to an open-mouthed public the most incredible feats of magic and yet, once the trick is revealed, we see that it was all sleight of hand and no magic was involved.
In a similar fashion, even the most improbable events discovered in life, if we know the trick, are just applied advanced physics.
The only possible exception being the creation of life itself.
Even this, common sense tells us that there must be a rational explanation to, but at the moment, we cannot see beyond the magic and so we are in the position of the open-mouthed public, completely baffled as to how the feat is achieved although we suspect that the secret will be revealed to us one day.
This is why we are so interested in these orbs.

The one we are studying and, by extension, all of them, seem to contain nothing connected to life and yet, once they come together, life is produced rather like a rabbit appearing from the magician's hat.

This puzzles us greatly and so we cogitate on what possible force can be contained within the orbs, that seem inert when contained within an individual orb, but that springs to life when all the orbs come together.

Once again, with the assistance of the advanced human archangels, we think we have the answer although explaining the technique to produce life is not going to be easy.
But we will try.

This is what we were told.

Life as we know it to be is not quite according to our understanding.
As we have previously stated, we have always considered that life was created as single dots in a kindergarten galaxy far away in time and space to our galaxy and each one of these dots of life were transferred to the 8th dimension of our multiverse where they wait patiently to be called onto the stage of life in some way, shape or form.

Indeed, we wrote a book about it and, rest assured, if we were not totally convinced that this is the truth as far as life in our sector is concerned, we would not have given you this information.
We do not speculate nor do we fabricate so we were and are convinced that what we told you is the truth.
But what we do not know was that, apparently, what we wrote is relevant to our existence but not to alternate realities like the one we are now considering.

This seems, at first, a bit strange. We know that the God of our multiverse created life as we stated it to be and, thus, we rather assumed that life everywhere would follow a similar pattern of creation.
This has taught us a valuable lesson.
We should never assume anything when investigating unknown matters but always look at the evidence and follow that evidence wherever it takes us.

In the case under discussion, let us follow the evidence and see where it does take us.
This requires an open mind and we will admit that it is as difficult for us to be open minded as it is for large numbers of you.

Perhaps you can understand that people who have lived in non-physicality for vast periods of time and, collectively and individually, have studied the science of life as it applies to our multiverse would find it difficult to be confronted with evidence in direct contradiction to any knowledge previously assimilated.
It is not easy to go back to square one and start again but this is what we are required to do if we wish to understand this aspect of life.
This is why, at the beginning of this book, we suggested that you would need to forget all that we had told you about life and start again.

This, of course, is not entirely true because, as we said, there are some aspects of life in this galaxy that correspond to some aspects in our galaxy.

But what we are suggesting is that the prime creative force has followed a different path to ours and thus we need to clear our mind and be prepared to accept new information.

Having stated all that to prepare you that we are heading into uncharted waters, let us try to explain to you that which was explained to us by these very advanced human archangels concerning this galaxy and this God's creative powers.

The first thing we learnt was, as we already knew, actually, was that there are a vast number of galaxies spread throughout what we might call the multiverse and that each one of these galaxies has an independent God creating life in various ways according to an overriding directive.

We need to explain this very important statement because it is totally new to you - and to many of us - and will change the way we consider life.
The part that is so important is the last line of the above sentence; according to an overriding directive.

What does that mean?
People have often questioned that if God exists, then who made God?
This question has been asked but never satisfactorily answered.
It is assumed that God just is!
God is the beginning of everything and it is pointless in questioning the origins of God.
God just is.

But now we are being presented with an expanded concept concerning God(s).

Let us look at the problem in a very simple way that we hope will shed some light on the answer.
Imagine a jigsaw puzzle.
It consists of many separate pieces, each one of which consists of a picture in its own right but it is not until the last piece is put in place that the picture is truly complete and truly revealed.
We are sure that you can visualise that.
But, we also realise that someone created the picture and cut out the individual parts into which the picture was divided.

Now, the person who made the jigsaw had no connection to the jigsaw other than he created it. By which we mean that the creator of the jigsaw puzzle was not a form of advanced jigsaw puzzle but was something entirely different: a human who desired to create a jigsaw puzzle.

When people mull over in their minds who created God or the Gods of other galaxies, it is usually assumed that the Creator would be a super version of God as we imagine it or them to be.
But, in the case of the creator of a jigsaw puzzle, we showed that the creator was human and has no direct connection to the jigsaw other than he created it. The creator is not a form of super jigsaw.

So, is it possible that the creator of all these different Gods is a form of intelligence and, if so, where does he/she/it exist and is it possible to identify with it to find out how it functions?

Then, of course, it begs the question; if there truly is an intelligence capable of creating God(s), who created that intelligence?
However, let us not get too ahead of ourselves.

If we can solve the problem of who or what created the various Gods, that will be a start.

You may have wondered why we mentioned a jigsaw puzzle?

If you can remember us mentioning the strange event of the galaxy only springing to life as and when the last orb existed, you can see the connection.
The jigsaw is only finished, complete, when the last piece is in position.
We readily admit that a jigsaw puzzle is not alive in any real sense but we hope you can appreciate the analogy.

Now, let us expand the concept.
We told you that in this galaxy, and no doubt others, life only sprang into existence when the last part of it connected to the whole and we used the analogy of a jigsaw not being complete until the last piece was in place.

We wish to suggest to you that there are a huge but finite number of galaxies each one with a God exploring a theme unique to itself. This may be a truly enormous number of galaxies and Gods but the number is finite.

We wish, further, to present to your consideration that it was only when they were all created did any of the Gods or the galaxies spring into creation.
This may seem most improbable but, apparently, is the truth.

There are a huge number of galaxies and a huge number of Gods, one for each galaxy, but none of them existed, neither Gods nor galaxies, until they all existed and then life everywhere sprang into being.

So we have a grandiose version of the Big Bang theory although we can only use that metaphor in a relative sense as we know that, in our galaxy, the world we live in was created by copying a previously existing galaxy in the seventh dimension.

The question that we cannot answer is whether the galaxy we are now examining was created as a copy/paste process from a previously existing galaxy like ours or was it created in a different fashion?
The problem is that just by looking at the galaxy as it is today gives us no indication as to its origins.

This is a problem that exists in all versions of physicality.
Just by examining what exists in physicality in our galaxy gives no real clue as to the origins of things, so science has to make wild assumptions, some of them close to the truth and some wide of the mark.

We could site the Big Bang theory as a wrong assumption along with the creation of life generally and humans in particular and yet, to this day, Big Bang and Darwinism are taught in schools and universities.
We have discussed this at length in various other publications but it saddens us to see how closed-minded scientists of all denominations can be.
We hope that, in time, science will start to open its eyes and look behind the scenes to find the truth.

But are we in a position to find the truth as to the origins of the universe under discussion?

Once again we turn to the wise archangels who inform us that many, indeed most, of the galaxies were created following a similar pattern.
So, if this is true, it assumes that this galaxy was created by a copy/paste idea from a previously created galaxy in a different dimension.

This, of course, opens doors to a plethora of other questions as to whether this galaxy has dimensions like ours, were the life forms born and raised in a kindergarten system like ours and so forth.

To answer these questions we need to turn to those who have the answers - the human archangels.

Let us compare what we know about our galaxy and the life forms that live in or on it and this new galaxy that we are trying to examine.

We have already given you a book that examined and explained how our galaxy was formed. Indeed, we explained how life in our galaxy was created in several of the books as all aspects of life are connected, so to talk about any aspect implies mentioning the connections to all aspects.
So, whether we are talking about DNA or talking about alien life, it is all connected.

But the question we need answering is does the life in the galaxy that we are currently examining have connections to our life in our galaxy?

The Archangels inform us yes and no - not very helpful we thought.
So, as we know that the archangels are trying to help us, we asked them to expand upon their answer.

They told us that there was some similarities and some dissimilarities between the way that our galaxy and this galaxy were constructed

The obvious similarities is that there is a God and this God has a theme (peace) and that all of it had to be in place, like the pieces of a jigsaw, before it all sprang to life.
A further similarity is that all the orbs collectively create the conditions for that life to be manifested just as it does in our galaxy.

However, one of the major differences is that we can find no evidence of individual life in any of the orbs despite there being overwhelming evidence that each orb is alive in some fashion.

We really must investigate this important difference and find how something can be alive despite there being no indication of where that life force is contained.

In our galaxy, as we have explained in a previous book, there is a life force that we called the logos and we also went to great lengths to describe the important role played by DNA in allowing that logos to circulate throughout all life in all living things.
But, in the case of these orbs we can find no logos nor can we find any DNA.
So, there is a fundamental, a radical difference between what we consider life to be and what life is in this galaxy we are investigating.

We can but seek the advice from the learned archangels that are informed concerning this galaxy.

What they tell us is somewhat difficult to comprehend as it is totally different from anything with which we are familiar.
But we will do our best to explain in simple terms.

In the case of this galaxy, what we call life is not contained within any orb.
The orbs are elements of a collective and it is the collective that forms a life force.

Please let us expand on this concept. The force we call God in this universe is the total of the life force and could, if it wished, exist in isolation from any orb in which to manifest itself.
In other words, it could represent the total, finished picture of the jigsaw, to refer back to a previous analogy.
But, at the same time, this God force decided to create these orbs for some purpose that is not clear to us.
Having created these orbs, it animates them rather as a puppeteer would manipulate a puppet.
So, the orbs are not directly alive in an individual sense other than the life that this God gives them.
So these orbs are both alive and not alive.
So it appears the life force of this God reaches out and provides the orbs with a limited amount of life force, not really sufficient to allow them to act as individuals but sufficient to act as a collective.
But, at the same time, this God could, if it so chose, supply any individual orb with sufficient power as to be able to act as if it was alive in an individual sense.

This is what happened when we decided to investigate an orb. The God force sensed our interest and thus gave this orb sufficient God force to be able to interact with us and thus, to us, it seemed alive in an individual sense.

This also is how, when the God force decided to interact with all the orbs to implant some information, it drew them all into a singularity.

This, as you can imagine is a new concept to us and we find this very interesting.

It is interesting in that, as all life is one, despite this God force acting in a very different way to our God force, there must be some connection to our God force.

So we need to investigate any connection to our way of life which we will do in the next chapter.

CHAPTER 7

THE JIGSAW PUZZLE

In the last chapter we noticed some fundamental differences between our galaxy and the galaxy we were investigating, notably the way that the God of the galaxy we were investigating and our God created life forces in our galaxy and the solo creative forces of the God under consideration.

This God, apparently, created orbs but did not endow these orbs with any life as opposed to our galaxy in which our God - via the Directors of Life - created countless stones, plants, animals and people, each one containing the Logos of life and each one having experiences which were passed back to our God so that it could grow in wisdom.

So, a moment's thought would enable us to realise that the God of the galaxy we were investigating had no means of growing in wisdom as it had no feedback from the orbs. Yet we consider that the feedback system, allowing our God to grow in wisdom, is a fundamental attribute of our God.

So, is it necessary for our God to grow in wisdom, or is it enough that God exists and has no need of more wisdom?
A tricky question and, if we can investigate the nature of God, it might shine some light on the true nature of what we call God and enable us to find out if there is some other intelligence behind and above these various Gods that we know about, an intelligence rather like the one we mentioned when we considered the creator of a jigsaw puzzle.

Once again, we need to draw a distinction between the God of religion and the God of creation.
We know, from experience, that the God of religion is prime creator, remote from any investigation and it is blasphemy to consider investigating it.

We must also say that the God of any religion is connected solely to planet Earth and the galaxy in which planet Earth is, and there is never any possibility investigation of any other Gods in other galaxies. If there was any investigation of any galaxies remote from ours, it would be assumed that it was our God that created it, something that our investigations suggest is not true.

We will say that there appears to be a connection between the various Gods but that they are independent of each other and are creator Gods in their own right.

We hope, eventually, to discover how these God's seem to act so differently to each other and why our God appears to want our life experiences and another does not.

So, we will devote this chapter to investigating the differences between the two Gods.

Suppose, for example, our God suddenly decided that it did not require to learn from our experiences.
What would happen to us?
At first thought we might suppose that all life as we know it would disappear.

As we have been told that God created all life so as to grow in wisdom through our experiences, we might well suppose that, if God no longer needed us, we would cease to exist.
But is this true?

Our investigations have led us to conclude that life would continue without sending the feedback to God. In other words, God does not require learning from our experiences. God exists in its own right, with or without our experiences, and we exist in our own right and do not rely on sending feedback to God in order for us to exist.

We fully accept that the God Logos is placed in association with us and it is that Logos that creates life.
But we do not agree, now, that God requires our feedback to it (God).
God can exist with or without us, and we can exist without sending that feedback to God.

Now, this appears to be a contradiction to all the teachings we have given you to say that feedback from us to God happens. But it is not.
Wisdom given to us by advanced beings has told us that our experiences are returned to God but that God does not need that feedback.
There is a difference between our experiences returned to God and God needing that experience in order to grow.
If that is so, then why are the results of our experiences returned to God?

The answer is that life is a chain and once an experience occurs, our reaction to that or those experiences need to create a link, a circle.
In other words, God sends out a life creating experience and it is our reaction to any experience that needs to return to the originator of that experience for the force to be reabsorbed into the creator and for the energy to be dissipated.

This is a difficult subject to understand.
We might say that the electrical energy sent down a wire needs to be used up by an electric machine in order for that energy to dissipate.
We could not have a situation where electric energy is sent down a wire and no machine use it up.
Electric energy cannot just remain in the wire.

So, in our galaxy, our God has put into place a system in which energy from that God is sent out to us and we need to use up that energy through our experiences which then returns back to the creator - God - and that provides our God with more energy to be sent out to create more experiences.

It is an endless cycle of energy being sent out, used up which, effectively, returns to God and that creates more energy to keep life going. It is an endless cycle.

Although this happens, we do not think that our God needs that energy.
It is just the manner that our God decided to put into place.
Our God could operate without any real contact with us and we could exist without the feedback loop also.

Thus, to repeat, we can state that our God could exist without the feedback loop from us and we could survive without the feedback loop to God.

But that loop is in place and so it operates.
Whether God actually learns from our experience is another matter.
Certainly, we agree that the energy returning to God liberates more energy but we strongly feel that we, without God, could use energy created by our Logos to provide us with experiences and once we have resolved those experiences more is liberated to create energy for the next experience.
So, once again, we have this conundrum, this dichotomy.
On one hand we have God sending us experiences and our reaction to these experiences being sent back to God to create more energy and, on the other hand, our Logos possibly sending us experience and then absorbing that energy to create more experience.

This seems strange, until we realise that our Higher Self is in contact with our Logos - our spirit of God - which, itself, is connected to almighty God.
Thus, whether our experiences are sent to almighty God or whether they are sent to our Logos via the Higher Self, as our Higher Self, of which there is only one, is connected to our Logos which, despite there being one for every living thing on Earth, as the various Logo are connected to God, it works out to be the same.

Can you see this?

There is one almighty God for our galaxy and there are countless individual spirits of God, one for each living thing connected via the one Higher Self to almighty God.
Thus, the Logo of each and every life spirit are connected to the one almighty God and could possibly share the results of our life experiences.
The Logo and the one God are, effectively, the same thing.

It is only the fact that God created a Logos for every living thing that created the need to share experiences and send them back to individual's Gods and God itself.
The Logos and God, effectively, being the same thing.

If we did not exist, almighty God could still exist and not require our feedback. Equally, under different circumstances, we could exist without needing to send feedback to the Logo.

It is just the way that life in our galaxy, that makes the feedback loop need to exist, that makes it so.

This is a very difficult thing to describe and we are not sure that all can understand but we have done our best to describe the process just using words.
If we had a black or white board at our disposition it would have made the description easier but we only have words.

So, to return to the galaxy that we will call the orb galaxy, we do not have such a complicated system as there is only really a God force.

Admittedly, this God maintains a connection to each orb but has no feedback system and has only a tenuous hold over each orb instead of a complex interplay between itself (almighty God) and the Logo, the individual versions of almighty God, divided into countless versions of itself, one for each Logos.

So, we hope you can see that this version of God, the orb God, has only a limited connection to our version of God and yet they are all Gods.
Logic would decree that the different Gods would all be the same but, clearly, they are not!

Now, we don't know how many galaxies there are in all, and thus we don't know how many versions of God there are, nor by what degree they vary, one from another, but it does seem strange to think that they may all vary, one from another.

If we consider, in our galaxy, how many different personalities there are amongst people, but they are all created by one God, one Higher Self, which is itself closely connected to almighty God, but all have individual versions of almighty God that we call Logos, it makes us wonder if, behind all these various Gods, there might be an overriding force - a sort of super God - rather like the creator of a jigsaw puzzle, that created all these Gods.

So, if we can visualise all the individual pieces of a jigsaw as all the various Gods, each one different but each one connected to the overall picture, we can imagine that behind each God is an overall God that creates a sort of complete picture of God, then we wonder what being made the various Gods, just like we wonder who created a jigsaw puzzle, each piece separate but, collectively, create an overall picture.

This is complicated so we will repeat the story.

Imagine a finite but varying concept of a large number of Gods of a number of galaxies, each God different but each God part of a complete number of Gods which, when they come together, form a picture of a super God.
Then, if this is so, it begs to find the being that created the Gods.
So, if we consider our God plus the God of the orb galaxy, that are just two Gods in a multiverse, and that each galaxy has an individual God, it is only when all the Gods are in place that we see the complete picture of what all the Gods create.

This might be considered to be a super God.
But then we realise that there must be some force that creates the various Gods that come together to create the overall God picture.

So, we have our God as just one of a number of Gods.
Then, when all the Gods are in place, there is a bigger picture, a sort of super God made of all the different Gods coming together.
Then, behind all this must be a grander force - intelligence - that created the super God.

The only way we can really describe all this is to think of a jigsaw puzzle, but think of it in reverse.
First there is an intelligence who wants to create a jigsaw puzzle. So, he gets a picture. Then the picture is cut up into small pieces.

It is only when we put all the pieces together again, that the picture is revealed and we think of the person who created it all.

So, if our logic is correct, there are at least three stages to life:
1. The individual Gods which, when they come together create;
2. A larger picture created by the individual Gods coming together, and;
3. A higher wisdom that created the whole thing.

We have enough problems visualizing just our God, so you can imagine how complex it is to investigate the total number of Gods and then to try to find out the intelligence that created all the Gods.
And yet we know that life tries to keep things simple, so we rather suspect that, if we can see behind the magic, the answer will be simple, assuming that our thinking is correct.

We have, at this moment, little to go on other than we have discovered two versions of God that seem to differ somewhat; our God and the orb God.

All the rest, for the moment, is speculation and yet something tells us we are on the right track if only we can see behind the magic to the physics involved.

The question is, of course, how do we investigate this complicated event? How could we possibly find out about the super God and then this prime intelligence that created the plethora of individual Gods?

Even the human Archangels that normally provide us with information have a limit to their knowledge so we cannot rely on them to provide us with an answer.

Fortunately, there is a means of finding an answer and that answer is contained within a part of the Akashic Record that we have mentioned before, a sort of restricted section that only a privileged few have access to.

There is a lot of information contained within the restricted reserve of the Akashic Record, that most people never get to see, as this area contains knowledge that it would not be good for all to know.
Under ordinary circumstances, people like us would not be given access to this area and we must say that this information concerning the various Gods and the creator of those Gods has never been revealed to anyone and so you who read this book will be given information never before revealed either to us or to people incarnate.

Permission has been granted because time is short, and it is important that you are all given as much information as possible before the next phase of life takes over.
This process is called Ascension and, as we have said, you cannot rise in spirituality until you have all the facts concerning life.

So, for the first time in modern Earth's history, we can reveal to you how this bizarre aspect of life works and how it was all created.

This we will start to do in the next chapter.

CHAPTER 8

THE DIVERSE PERSONALITIES

In the last chapter we introduced the strange concept of multiple intelligences, God after God, each one more creative than the others.
We suggested that there was a creative force that made a large number of Gods that would need to come together to form a super God.
By that we implied a large number of individual Gods that needed to join forces in order to create a super God and, from that super God, all the individual Gods of all the individual galaxies were created.

This is a difficult concept to describe effectively because we are suggesting that all the individual Gods, including our God, needed to be created and it was only when all the Gods were created that they came together to form, from the individual Gods, a combination of all the Gods that formed a super God, created by and from all the Gods being created.

The only way we could effectively describe this was to use the example of a jigsaw puzzle where a complete picture was cut up into many small pieces and each piece needed to be put back together to reform the original picture. Then, and only then, could all the pieces reveal the original picture.

So we are suggesting that all the Gods need to be created before coming together which actually creates a bigger version of life and with it, individual Gods that could not exist until all were created.
We think that you will agree that this is very difficult to describe as we need all the Gods to be individually created and come together before any of the Gods could exist.
It is a bit like the question of which came first, the chicken or the egg?
To create the chicken we need an egg and to create an egg we need a chicken. Actually, we need two chickens - a male and a female - in order to create a fertile egg.

So, to create individual Gods - one for each Galaxy - we need them all to exist but for them all to exist as individual Gods, we need them all to exist as a collective already.

The only way to resolve this problem, it seems to us, is to have an overriding intelligence that created them all just like the person who takes a picture and cuts it up into pieces. The picture is still there but cut into pieces and it is only when they come back together again that they create the original picture.

So, our job is to find out who or what this overriding intelligence is and where it comes from.

This may, at first glance, seem to be an impossible task.

How can we even imagine a force capable of creating a vast number of Gods because it implies not only a force capable of creating Gods but, by the same token, capable of creating, at least in principle, in theory, all the subsections that go to make life in any area.

For instance, if we consider just our galaxy, not only do we have a God but we have archangels that put into creation all the dimensions and the countless, complicated life forms that have all been created.

Now, this implies that either this overriding intelligence, this master creator, had all this in mind when he created our galaxy or he (it) endowed our God with the creative power that enabled our God to formulate and put into action the incalculable number of marvels that go to make up all life as we know it to be in our galaxy without us even considering all the other marvels created by or in conjunction with the Gods of all the other galaxies.

Who amongst us could even consider such an entity?

Then, of course, we have to face the dreaded questions of what does this entity look like, if he has any form, and where does he come from, where does he live and, most dreaded question of all, who made him?

We call this master creative force "him" just because it is considered normal to refer to God in the masculine. If that offends you, please refer to this overriding force as she, it or any other appellation you care to give it.
We do not wish to offend anyone but we must refer, if we wish to discuss this entity, by some term. So we call it "he".

As we stated previously we have the restricted area of the akashic record that comes to our rescue and gives us some answers. Enough answers for us to be able to put two and two together to describe the makeup of this extremely complicated creation system.

Now, we did say, at the end of the previous chapter, that we would attempt to describe the master creator but, to do so, we need to make sure that we understand the effects of creation rather than describing prime creator and then hope to connect that to the various effects that are manifested.

So, the first thing we need clearly to understand is that there are a finite but large number of Gods, similar to ours in creative force, everyone in charge of creating a galaxy somewhere.

Our galaxy - universe, multiverse - call it what you will, has been created by our God who chose as his creative theme, love.

We have, in various books, talks and lessons, attempted to describe at least some of what our God created and although what we have described is just a drop in the ocean compared to what we could say in reference to the creative power of our God, we hope that you can see that what God has created is truly amazing and it requires a real stretch of the mind to accept it.

If we go back to the concept of the jigsaw puzzle, if there was just our God, the complete jigsaw picture would show just an image of our God, assuming that Gods can be seen.

So, once again we ask you to accept what we are saying metaphorically and that the picture of God in the jigsaw puzzle is hypothetical. God cannot really be seen. It is an imaginary picture.

But, we mentioned another galaxy that we referred to as the "orb galaxy" and said that there was a God force in charge of that galaxy. We discovered that the motivating force of the orb galaxy was peace.
So that would give us two pictures in a jigsaw, one of love and a second of peace.
Now, we stated that these two Gods were independent of each other but were, at the same time, connected as part and total of the jigsaw picture.

Obviously, if we were able to investigate the orb galaxy more thoroughly, we would discover other similarities between it and our God but it suffices for the moment to accept that there is more than just our God in creation and each God can create independently from our God although there always remains a connection between the Gods. A connection that we won't, for the moment, describe.

So far we have put into our jigsaw puzzle two pictures, if you will allow us to continue to use this analogy. So this points us in the direction of the creative force that created the two Gods.
If there was only one God for all of creation that would simplify matters but the fact that we know that there are more than one creator God implies a force higher and above God that creates Gods in the plural.

Before we attempt to describe this higher force, let us continue to fill our jigsaw image with sufficient visages of Gods so as to complete the picture.
We have admitted that we do not know the exact number of Gods there are nor do we know the number of galaxies but we do know that, for each galaxy, there is a creator God and we also know that each God has a theme that he acts upon.

We assume that some force has decided how many themes exist in creation - love, hate, peace, war etc., - and has created a God and a galaxy to explore each and every aspect that could be created.
Therefore, we assume that some higher force has considered each and every aspect of creation and has created a God and a galaxy to explore all of the aspects of consciousness that exist.

So, just as we have people on Earth that reflect all of the possible aspects of thought, of being, of reactions to life so there are Gods and galaxies that also reflect the same themes.

This is curious because, although the theme of our God and all his creation is love, nevertheless we find people that display, individually, all of the aspects of emotion possible.
By which we mean that there are people here on Earth and also in the various dimensions, that display love, hate, peace, war, fear, compassion and all of the aspects of emotion that exist.

This seems somewhat confusing as logic would decree that, as the theme of our planet is love, we would only find loving people on our planet and any people who display other emotions would have been born into a galaxy that explored the emotion corresponding to the emotion of that person.
In other words, those who are loving would be born here but those who are hateful, or fearsome, or compassionate or whatever, would be attracted to the galaxy the God of which would explore the same theme.

So all this seems rather strange.

On one hand we have all these galaxies and Gods, each one dedicated to exploring a particular theme or emotion but, at the same time, we have here on Earth a mixture of people who display the very same emotions.

Now, we don't know for sure if there are entities that only follow the theme of their God but we can state with certainty that the people on or around planet Earth display a mixture that are not, necessarily, only displaying the emotion of love.
Indeed, there are many who seem to be in opposition to love.

So, what does this tell us?

What inference can be drawn from the fact that people here on Earth or in the astral dimensions surrounding Earth can be of any type of emotion?

Can we infer that the galaxies and Gods of other areas are closely connected to the people attracted to planet Earth?

This seems to be getting stranger and stranger because either planet Earth seems to be a special case unconnected to the other galaxies and Gods or, in some way, the other galaxies and Gods are totally connected to the people of Earth, including all those in various dimensions.

Can you understand what we are suggesting?

Our investigations have revealed that there are a large but finite number of galaxies and Gods remote from Earth, each one of which is dedicated to exploring a particular theme or emotion and that there is one God and one Galaxy for each emotion. But, at the same time, here in our galaxy there are people who also respond to each emotion.

So, logic would suggest a close connection to each galaxy and its God and the people of Earth who respond to the very same emotions that the various Gods and galaxies purport to study.

It is almost as if planet Earth is acting as a sort of capture point, a clearing house to all the various galaxies and Gods apparently devoted to the study of the various emotions.

This seems to defy logic.

If the theme of our galaxy and God is love how can it be that the people of our galaxy can show such diverse emotions?
Also, if all these other galaxies and Gods, each one exploring a particular theme, explore the same themes as the people of our galaxy, it is almost as if these strange galaxies and Gods are in some way connected to the people of our galaxy.

But, if this was so, it would imply that the people of our galaxy were also connected to the galaxies and Gods of these various themes.

It seems to imply that every person alive connected to planet Earth is also connected to one of the other galaxies and Gods, the connection being the emotional theme; peace, harmony, hate, cruelty and all the diverse emotions.

We will repeat this in slightly other words.
We have discovered, dispersed throughout the multiverse, a large but finite number of galaxies, each one under the control of a God and each God exploring an emotional theme.

But, at the same time we know that, in the multiverse connected to our God, there are a similar number of people (Logo) exploring a similar number of themes.

This seems to imply that each one of us is not only connected to our galaxy but, at the same time, is closely connected to another galaxy and another God according to how we react to emotions; love, hate, compassion, etc.

To cut a long story short, it implies that people (Logo) are not only connected to our galaxy in all its dimensions but, at the same time are connected to the various Gods and galaxies exploring the various emotional themes.
We draw the conclusion that, if we go back to the concept of a jigsaw puzzle and if we could create a picture of each God as a piece of the jigsaw, each part, each face of a God would represent an aspect of emotion as lived by the people that go to make up the people of our galaxy.

This has strange ramifications.
It implies that the people alive in our galaxy have a particular personality because the overriding master force created them all as part of this jigsaw but, when applied to people (Logo) decided to put them in our galaxy.

It is as if the galaxies and Gods that go to make up the jigsaw are just creations but those creations come to life when adopted by humans in our galaxy.

It also implies that our God has one part of creation under its wing but the galaxy and God promoting any one aspect of emotion also plays a role in promoting a personality aspect of a human.

This seems to be extremely complicated. And it is, until one can comprehend the concept of various Gods creating people - or rather, personalities - while another God (our one), creates people.
So, our God creates people (Logo), while the personalities of those people are created by other Gods in other galaxies.
It implies that live people and their personalities are two separate aspects of life.

We want you to understand this because it is new information never before revealed - at least to the population of Earth this time around. So we will explain it all again in clearer terms.

We want you to understand that the God of our multiverse created one person - just one - and put the Logos of himself with that one person.
But he (God) also endowed that Logos to imagine that it was a huge number of people.
But, without any personality, it would be obvious that there was only one person. It is personality that creates conscious life.
So, please understand that this master intelligence created our God who, in turn, creative one life force.
Then, this master intelligence created a number of other Gods, each one exploring an aspect of personality, of emotion.

Now, this is where it gets difficult to describe.

The master creator took the one logos of our God and divided it up into a number of parts and put a part with each personality creating God so that, now, not only do we appear to have a large number of people but each one of these people have a distinct personality.
It is these personalities that create conscious life.
That is why independent life could only exist when all the independent Gods had been created, each one influencing a certain proportion of the one logos.
These diverse Gods needed all to be created so as to be able to divide the one logos into many parts, each part containing a distinct personality.

So, if we have understood correctly, we have a master creative force that created our God rather like a queen bee or a queen ant and then, for each and every aspect of personality, a series of Gods and galaxies in order to give personality to aspects of the one logos.
It is personality that gives life to the divided-up logos.

We could, before we try to discover more about this dual existence, attempt to find out why all living things are attracted to planet Earth and its various dimensions.
The answer is simple and we have mentioned it many times.
Planet Earth the only one in which there is physical life and the dimensions around planet Earth are the only ones in which complete humans - body, personality and soul - come together.

Why planet Earth was chosen as the melting pot for all life we cannot say.
We can only acknowledge that it is so.
Had another planet, another galaxy been chosen, the outcome would have been the same so it matters not what planet system was chosen.

What is important is to realise that life, particularly human life, is split into two parts. One part is the life we live on Earth and in the dimensions surrounding Earth and the second part is to realise that each and every life logos has a personality and these personalities group and develop in and around other galaxies elsewhere.
There are various personality types and these personalities group in one area, a galaxy for each personality.

Thus we have bodies and then personalities.
Eventually we must decide how the bodies and the personalities link together and if they ever actually join or if they remain apart.

This will be the subject of the next chapter.

CHAPTER 9

THE PLANETS OF PERSONALITY

You may remember that we discovered and explored, to a certain extent, one of the personality galaxies and its creative God.
We could call it the orb galaxy because it seemed to be a galaxy containing just a vast number of, apparently, lifeless orbs.
We further discovered that the theme of the God of this galaxy was peace and, when it drew all the orbs into a singularity, stressed that it wanted the orbs to explore and appreciate the concept of peace.

With hindsight, now that we have learnt more about these galaxies, we can appreciate that what we were involved with was a galaxy and a God that was created to explore the concept of peace.
We stress that it was purely by haphazardness that we discovered one that explored peace.
It could have been any emotion that we stumbled across.
And we suggest that the experience would have been similar.
So let us describe what we saw, what we deduce and, finally, what we know about this orb galaxy and, by extension, all the personality creations.

We mentioned a galaxy that contained a huge number of orbs.

We said that there was no evidence that these orbs were alive in the sense that we are but we realised that life can take many forms and we should not jump to the conclusion that just because something does not seem to contain life as we know it, it is not alive

It also teaches us to dig deeper and investigate where life leaves off and non-life starts.
We used this phrase 'non-life' because, in fact, as you should be aware by now, nothing can die but we do appreciate that some things seem more alive than others.
For instance, if we look at a forest in full flower, it is obviously full of life, but if we look at the same forest after a devastating fire although it can be argued that the fauna and flora have just changed form, to our eyes it seems to have lost most of its life.

Now, if we examine all the life forms in our galaxy; plants, animals and people, we can see what is obviously alive and what is not.
But if we look at the orbs in the orb galaxy we can find no evidence of obvious life.

This, we now realise is because each orb is not so much life but an aspect of personality.
This is interesting because we said previously that a logos (a living thing) can only spring to life when its personality is attached to it and yet, if we examine pure personality, it does not seem to contain life in any visible way.

But there are a few things we can deduce from the intelligence given to us by the very wise archangels who have access to the restricted area of the akashic record.
One of the things is that, if we could count the exact number of orbs in this orb galaxy, that would tell us how many people there are in our galaxy that have peace as their theme for life.

However, the problem is that many of us have a multiplicity of personality aspects to our make-up, not just one theme.

For instance, many of us have peace in our personality makeup but that does not stop us having other aspects as well; love, calmness, compassion, understanding and many other kind aspects.
We might also have other personality trends as well; short tempers, a certain degree of hate, bigotry and other somewhat negative bits to us.

How many of us can truly say that we only have one aspect of personality? Very few, we would suggest.

If this is true, and it surely must be, it implies a very complex mixture of which personality galaxies we can correspond to.
So, this raises yet another problem, a set of questions we must try to answer.

If we all had just one personality trend to our makeup, this aspect of life would be simple. Let us try to look at this in a basic fashion.

We now know that there exists in our galaxy - just to consider humanity - a number of different types of humans, some male, some female, some who appear to be in the wrong body. Some tall, some short, those with different skin colours and so on. A true plethora of people with different physical features.

Now we have discovered that each and every one of these people have, attached to them, personalities that come from a different galaxy.

This master creator, that we have yet to discover, for some reason best known to himself, decided to create galaxies and Gods and put into those galaxies something - at least in the case of one of them - that appear to be all that contain personalities.

So far, so good. Although it seems somewhat complicated, at least we can understand how personalities are created.

But we don't know how personalities are distributed to people, why, and just to complicate matters further, we know that most people have multiple bits of personality. So, to find the answers to these questions is going to take quite a bit of delving.

We will ignore for the moment the different physical attributes that we all have and concentrate our efforts on trying to discover the complexities of personalities.

We will also just concentrate on humanity because if we start to analyse all of life; stones, plants and animals, we will get lost in a maze of information.
In fact, we did touch, slightly, on the aspects of minerals, plants and animals in a previous book but we deliberately kept our investigations slight because we very quickly started to discover that life generally and personalities in particular were closely connected to DNA. We gave you a book on the subject.

Now, we mentioned in the book about DNA that much of it was invisible and was referred to as junk DNA.
We implied that DNA was of extreme importance and was second in importance only to life itself.

So, we have a strong suspicion that if we investigate personalities of people, we will find DNA playing a role.

We have to add another branch to our investigations.
We discovered a number of Gods, galaxies and aspects of personality (whether they be orb shaped or any other shape) and now we are suggesting that DNA is probably playing an important role somewhere in the story.

This is where we have to say that we are grateful for having presented the various books we gave you in the order we have because, if you have read all the books you will have a fairly clear knowledge of some of the aspects of personalities and will be able to piece together with us the jigsaw we are attempting to put together.

As we have just mentioned, DNA always seems to be involved with life somewhere and, in the book on aliens, we mentioned that some aliens are actually unused personality bundles assuming an independent life in the astral realms for a while.

We have, somehow, to try to draw these disparate aspects together to make sense of personality.

We will say that our ultimate goal in this book is to locate and understand somewhat this Master Creator, if we can, but we know from experience that we will not be able to do this if we have not some degree of mastery of life both physical and non-physical.

Therefore, it seems to be important to us to try to understand these personality spheres and their Gods and how they all link to life in our galaxy.

We have discovered, with the invaluable help with our archangelic mentors, that each orb galaxy and its God promotes one pure aspect of personality quite independent from any other orb galaxy.

We need really to understand this. Of all the huge but finite number of galaxies and Gods there are concerned with personality, each one helps create one pure aspect of personality, ignoring all the rest.

So, let us try to discover who and what is creating these pure aspects and why they are being focused in and on any one galaxy to the exclusion of any other.
After all, we seem to be born with a variety of aspects of personality quite naturally and have suggested that they are, in some way, connected to our DNA.
This is all very well but doesn't answer any questions as to why we have personalities in the first place?
If we have personalities, they must be created somewhere and for some reason.

In a previous book we mentioned the links we could locate between minerals, plants, animals and humans and suggested that each species; mineral, plant, animal etc., started with the same basic attributes but, as consciousness evolved, species by species, so we added more and more levels of awareness according to the species. For instance, it would be fairly obvious that the average human has higher levels of awareness than the average animal.

This does not imply that a human is any better than any animal but it does imply that most humans require a higher level of intellectual capacity to deal with daily life than the average animal.
One could say, of course, that an animal can survive in the wild whereas most humans deposited in the wild would struggle.

The point we wish to make to you is that you, if you read the book that mentioned personalities of minerals, plants, animals and, eventually, humans, they all started with the same basic attributes but each species added more and newer ones according to his species.
A plant has more attributes than a stone. An animal has more than a plant. At the top of the list is humanity, or will be one day.
So we must assume that personality is linked to consciousness and varies according to the species.

Why should this be? Where does it all start and how is personality manufactured because, if we all have personalities, which are connected to consciousness and all this is connected to DNA, some entity must have decided to create it.
As we have often said, there is no such thing as magic. Everything is based on physics in one way or another.

To understand how personality was and is created is very deep physics indeed but, fortunately, we don't need to cover black boards with hieroglyphics not invent a mass of new words.
We can explain just using plain English.

Life, as we have said in the past, has always existed.

We did try to explain that the word 'always' is a misnomer because time does not exist and therefore 'always' just means 'now'.

This is a difficult concept to grasp because even you who are reading this book will born at sometime in the past and most of you have a birth certificate to prove it and, depending on your age, you can remember going to various schools, may have had a variety of jobs etc.
These events trace your life from the moment of your birth up until now and will go on until the end of your incarnation on Earth.
So, you have the concept of life continuing day after day ever onwards inculcated in you from the moment of your birth until the moment of your release from incarnation.
At that point everything changes because once you return to your home in the Heavenly spheres time no longer has any relevance.
Time, and indeed, space are only associated with incarnation.
All people in the heavenly spheres are immortal.
You are immortal.

But we, or rather you, are incarnate and thus have to deal with apparent space/time.
It is no use pretending that space and time do not exist in so-called 3D reality (incarnation), because they do.

This is where things start to get very complicated.

The almighty power(s) that created all life had, eventually, to create life in two manners or fashions.

We have explained in other works that humanity was not originally designed to come to Earth. Earth was created for minerals, flora and fauna.
However, when it proved that these entities were not sufficient, humans were introduced.

This dramatically changed everything because humans are much different from even the most advanced animals.
Humans have levels of awareness, of consciousness that no animal could achieve.
We will say, at the risk of insulting you, that the humans that incarnate at the moment and in the past are only a primitive form of human. In the future, as we move more fully into ascension, so an advanced race of humans will be introduced.
These humans are being prepared even now and, when the time is ripe, will be introduced.
The humans will be at the level of Jesus or Buddha or of the other great Masters and many of them will be even more advanced.

You may remember Jesus saying, "These things I do, you will do, and more."
That is what he was referring to.

But, in the meantime, we have to take things slowly and we had our incarnations and you are now going through yours.

We may not be at the level of the great Masters who will come here but we all do our best.

There is a logic to this slow progression from primitive people to very wise ones.
It may be thought that if all new arrivals on Earth were very wise, noble and peace-loving people, life would dramatically change and peace would reign.
This is not so.
We were, for a long time, in the negative swing of the pendulum of life and evil had full sway.
Now, as you should know, we are gradually moving into ever more positive moments but we are not fully there yet.
Evil forces are being chased from the theatre of life but, as most people are aware, the evil ones are clinging on and keeping as great a stranglehold on all aspects of life as possible.
Both they and we know that their battle is lost and they will, one day, depart the scene but, we must wait patiently for things to alter.

So, what has all this got to do with personalities?

Let us go back to a time we mentioned in a previous book, before you were incarnated. Obviously, we mention you but that is just to get your attention and make the story more interesting. You, in fact, refers to all of us, past, present and future.

Before you incarnated, we mentioned that you were taken on tours of the heavenly and hellish spheres of the higher 4th dimension, where we all live, and shown what was going on there.
Your friends, guides, teachers and mentors noted your reactions to the events you were shown and careful note taking of your interests.

So, comparing notes, they built a list of those events you found interesting and those that did not interest you.
Obviously, you took an active part in the discussions.

Eventually, as the date for your incarnation drew closer, you began to leave the school areas of heaven and were introduced to a number of areas that exist that help shape personality.

People are aware of some of these areas and they are called the signs of the zodiac.

In the night sky, certain clusters of stars have been given names in an attempt to quantify aspects of personality and are called Pisces, Aries, Taurus, Sagittarius etc., - twelve galaxies in all.
Obviously, and we don't wish to offend anyone, these star clusters have absolutely no connection to what is really happening behind the scenes but we do not ridiculise the

concept because it describes in a very accurate way what is going on in the spiritual realms.
So it does help to explain personalities.

However, as we have explained before, embryo spirits are moved down the dimensional layers, closer and closer to Earth until, finally, they end up - or perhaps it would be more accurate to say the personality aspect of them does - and arrive at one of the galaxies that we have been describing that we called the orb galaxies.

These galaxies correspond to the twelve signs of the Zodiac with which most people are familiar.

So, one of these galaxies will give a basic personality to an individual that we called Pisces, Aries, Capricorn etc.
However, as we mentioned, very few people have just one aspect of personality.
Many, indeed most, people have a mixture that astrologists get round describing by including influence from other star systems that they call houses etc.

In fact, there are a far larger number of orb galaxies than just twelve, so the angelic beings that still have the embryo human under their control introduce the young human to all of the galaxies that their teachers had noticed interested the baby human.

So, the personality aspects of this young person finishes up with a main personality aspect but with a variety of sub-aspects added.

One could perhaps compared it to a school system where a student would study a main subject, say mathematics, but would also study other subjects; English (or his native language), foreign languages, physics, sport or whatever.
So the student would leave school and enter the real world qualified as a mathematician but would also have a certain mastery of a number of other subjects.
What we all go through - or rather our personalities do - is very similar.
So, we have a main personality but a number of sub personalities also.

But we haven't really described what a personality is and why we need them.

Once again we are entering deep physics and going far beyond what conventional science, physics or even psychology or astrology are aware of. So we will introduce these concepts and just let you accept or reject what we tell you.

Let us ask you a question.
What is personality?

You all have personality which you might describe as likes and dislikes, desires, needs, wants, and you might, if you were courageous, connect personality to your ego, but could you really describe personality in any satisfactory sense?

A glance at a good dictionary will give some indication but many honest dictionaries state that there is no generally agreed upon definition of personality.

This is strange because we all have personality.
We stated that life without personality would be meaningless.
It is personality that separates man from machine.
Most animals have distinct personalities once one gets to know them and we could suppose that even plants have some form of personality.
It is most obvious in humans and yet dictionaries, or rather the people who write dictionaries, struggle to define personality.

Perhaps this is because the human being is composed of two distinct aspects.
One is connected to physicality and the other is connected to personality.
It is far easier to understand what we call physicality then personality.

For a start, much of what we call physicality is visible. We can see a human body, or an animal's body, or a plant and even a mineral and all these have been studied for many long ages.
We can see what we call life and death by which we mean, just to look at humanity, that a person either appears alive or dead.
We can study the organs, heart, lungs, spleen, liver and on and on and we can transfer information concerning people to students who, in turn, can teach others.
Thus, life seems fairly easy to comprehend.

But when we start to investigate personality, things become much more difficult to understand.

The first problem is that there is nothing practical (physical) that we can see or identify with.

As we said, with regard to the physical aspects of a person, just by looking at someone we can make some assumptions as to their race, sex, and a number of attributes. This helps put people in boxes if you see what we mean and we all like to be able to quantify plants, animals, minerals and people. It gives us the impression that we are in control of life.
But, with regard to personalities it is rather more difficult.
Most people find it difficult to define a person's personality until the person is well known to the questioner.

Of course, to those who have studied esoterics, it suffices to come close to an individual and the true nature of the person - his personality - is instantly revealed because we are all broadcasting our personality out through our auras all the time.
This is because we are all one and so, when we know how, we can link auras and thus link personalities.

So, what we are saying is that we all finish up with a mixture of personality, a main one that we chose to be incarnated with and a variety of sub personalities.
The reason that we need this mixture is, if we only had one personality, one theme that we explored, life would be very difficult. We would be like people who have a one-track mind.

Can you imagine if twelve people gathered together to discuss a problem and each one of them only had access to one aspect of personality, it would make agreement on a subject very difficult.
It is because we can draw on the various aspects of personality we all have that correspond to other people's personalities that we can see their point of view and thus agree on a subject or problem.

This, of course, opens the question as to why we have a main personality at all?
Would it not be better if we all had access to the twelve main traits and thus all act as one?

We have mentioned this before and have explained that we, at this stage of our evolution, are not sufficiently advanced as to be able to incorporate more than one main aspect of personality into us.
Long into the future, man will incarnate with all aspects of personality incorporated.
At that point man will live in peace with his fellow man and with all life as all men will think as one.
But we are not there yet so the best we can do is have a main personality and incorporate as many subpersonalities as possible which at least opens the door to accepting other people's points of view.

Of course, it makes it easier if the people we are interfacing with have an open mind as well. Conversation with people who have a closed mind on any subject quickly becomes impossible.
We see this in science and religion where people refused absolutely to consider an alternative point of view.

So where are we with all this?

Some master creator, long ago, decided to create life and created, with the help of trusted archangels, a number of Gods and planets (galaxies).
Into each one of these planets, he placed a God and gave that God a desire to explore a theme; love, hate, peace, war etc., as we have explained.
This master creator did exactly the same with our God and our galaxy and, by chance, gave our God love as his theme.

But this master creator went further. He decided to create life.

Quite what connection the master creator made between creating galaxies, Gods and life we do not really have the answer to but it does not take much of a stretch of the

imagination to realise that this master creator would not go to the trouble of creating countless galaxies and Gods if there was nothing left to play with.
So, life was his stroke of genius.
If it were not for the master creator deciding to create life, none of us would be here.

So, before we bring this chapter to a close, let us say that, at some point, our galaxy and our God was persuaded to act as home to life as we know it in addition - or, perhaps we could say as a replacement for - just being there waiting to introduce people to the concept of peace.

Therefore, the situation we are in now is that basic life is under the control of the God of life in all its vast variety of forms and the other galaxies are left with giving personalities to all those lifeforms, including us.

So, we hope that you can see that our God has taken you under his wing to help you become whatever you are, in your case a human.
You could have been a mineral, a plant, and animal, a drop of water or anything else but, thanks to the archangels by chance selecting you, you became a human - the pinnacle of this master creator's inventions.

CHAPTER 10

THE CREATION OF PERSONALITY

We have, thus far, made some attempt to explain that life generally and human life in particular is split into two parts - body and personality.

We have also gone to some lengths to explain that life is all illusion and the only thing that really exists is consciousness. Thus, life equates to consciousness.

We have also explained that personalities are created in separate galaxies, each one under the command of a God who was tasked with promoting one aspect of personality, which we linked to the signs of the zodiac, of which there are just twelve, although we explained that there are a large number of other aspects to personality, each one under the control of a God.
Finally, we explained that our galaxy, whilst it had a theme to explore - love - had also been tasked with raising all life that we might consider physical: minerals, plants, animals and humans.

We have not delved very deeply in this book, so far, to the vital role played by DNA. We mentioned it but have not really linked it in this book to just how vital DNA is, although we did explore its importance in another book we gave you about DNA.
Now, we have a problem because we do not like to repeat ourselves, and those who have read and understood the book on DNA should be able to link the importance of DNA to this book about physicality and personalities.

However, we wish to be polite and we must accept that many of you who are reading this book may well not have read the book on DNA or might not have retained all the aspects of it, so, if we may, we will devote this chapter to how DNA plays a role in the development of life.

We have stated that DNA is second only to the creation of life itself. This is no exaggeration.
If DNA did not exist, life would not exist.

We are not referring to the crude DNA tests police and science uses to compare blood or tissue samples.
We refer to the wonderful DNA science rejects as junk DNA.
Although we have described this DNA at some length before, we will start again and, if we can, we will link it to this book in a way that was not explained before.
So, we will not mention what we might call physical DNA at all.
It is the DNA that is working behind-the-scenes linking all aspects of life together that interests us.
So, where to start?

We have mentioned physical life and how it is created. Or perhaps we haven't.
Let us start again just with humans.

We explained, in a previous book, 'The Dawns of Life', that basic life was created in a kindergarten, and these points of life were eventually transferred to the eighth dimension of our galaxy.

Eventually, archangels gave a logos of life to them and gave them a unique identity. This might have been anything but, in your case and ours, it was the logos of human life.
Thus, you and we became humans.

Before you had a logos given to you, you were a point of life - a singularity - but that life was without any denomination. It was just life, if we can thus describe such a wonderful creation.
However, archangels gave you something that is referred to as a logos.
That logos tells you what you are destined to become.
That could have been a grain of sand, a drop of water, a plant, an animal of any description or a human.
By chance, you were given the logos of a human.
But the question is what is a logos?
What is it that tells you that you are a human instead of anything else?
The logos is DNA.
The word logos refers to DNA.
Now, each and every aspect of DNA is unique in several ways, it not only implies that you are human as opposed to a raindrop, an animal or anything else, but that DNA is ascribed exclusively to you and creates exclusively you.

So, when an archangel reached into the bank of life and selected a point of life, a singularity, it gave that point of life something we call a logos which actually means it gave that point of life DNA which not only told that point of life that it was going to be human but that it was going to be you.

Can you understand this?

At one point you were just a point of life which is a singularity.
This implies that, in reality, there is only one point of life.
We have not really explained this in quite this fashion before because we have to explain things slowly.
We are now at the point that we must explain things in a more exact fashion and hope that you can follow.

So try to imagine all basic life as a singularity in the eighth dimension.
A singularity, as you should know by now, appears as an almost invisible dot of consciousness although, if you have followed this book so far, you will know can consist of a vast number of living things but reduced in size to an unmeasurably tiny dot.

The archangels reached into that tiny dot, extracted a tiny portion of life and attached to it some DNA that corresponded to you and you were created.

Now, we must ask where did the DNA come from that created you?

This is the miracle.
Long before you were who you have become, you were created as DNA in a kindergarten that we have described in a previous book.
Then, eventually, you were transferred with countless others into the eighth dimension of our galaxy.
But you were not only DNA. You were given the spark of life.
Now, this DNA was not human at that point. That DNA is part of basic life.
But, when a human was needed, the archangels took the basic life form, complete with its DNA and added a final component that had been stored awaiting your moment, added it to the DNA and it all became you.

So, just what is this final piece of DNA that creates you?
This final piece is DNA that contains the components of your personality.

Thus, if we can start to link this together, you - just to consider you - are a point of life, given to you by archangels but created by God.
This point of life is what we refer to as a singularity and implies that everything that has ever been created, or ever will, is this tiny spark of life, this singularity that implies that there is only one tiny spark of life for all things.
That is why we constantly tell you that all is one.
It is because everything, at its origin, is created by this one, single point of life (a singularity).

The outreach of this is phenomenal if we can understand it. All things, whatever they are, exist because they all contain this one, tiny spark of life.
It is something that few people really stop to consider but the result of everything being created, at its base, from one identical dot of life implies that absolutely everything is the same.
Not only people, plants, animals etc., but galaxies, planets, space, time and absolutely everything are all just this one dot of life created by God.

Even this is not absolutely true in the sense that there is more to the story of creation than that but we will deal with that step later.

Let us, for the moment, try to accept that everything that has existed, exists now and will exist forever in the future, in all dimensions, has, at its base, this one unique life force. A tiny dot we call life but that we could also call consciousness.

However, as we have mentioned, there is more to life than just this spark of life.

It was decided that life as we know it was necessary to be created in order to make life more interesting.
After all, one tiny dot of life might well be a wonderful creation but does not create a very interesting life for anyone, God and the master creator included.

So, first, all the various galaxies and Gods that we have so far described in this book were created.
When all this was completed, our galaxy was chosen for a special task and that task was to house life.

So, the master creator thought about this and decided to create all the countless life forms that now exist. These were all to be placed in the care of our God.

The next problem was how to create all these objects from the one spark of life.

This is where something called DNA was invented.
Quite what being invented DNA we do not for the moment know.
It might well have been the master creator or the archangels that work for him or it might have been our God. We do not know but what we do know is that all that now exists was created in thought form, partly from the spark of life and partly from something we call DNA.

So what is DNA?
We have tried to explain DNA before in other books and lectures but we will briefly repeat again what it is.
We are not going to mention physical DNA that science studies but the much more interesting and so-called junk DNA.
This type of DNA is invisible as it is non-physical but exists in a variety of fashions.

The sort that interest us in this book is a type of DNA that tells each object what it is destined to become: a mineral, plant, animal, human, air, water or even gravity (amongst a large variety of other things).

So the master creator, no doubt in conjunction with his trusted cohorts, the archangels, took points of life and link them to a sort of design, a pattern, a meaning.
This design we call DNA and was linked to life in order to create life as we know it.

So, at this point, we have two aspects to life:
1. The actual spark of life without which nothing can exist.
2. DNA, which although not actually alive, nevertheless has sufficient life-force to tell the, now, 'object' what it is destined to be: a mineral, a plant, an animal and so on.
This DNA has a further aspect to it in that it not only tells the object that it is going to be, for example, an animal but which sort of animal it is going to be.
By which we mean a horse, a pig, a mouse, a snail or any other sort of animal.

So, at this point we have the concept of a created 'something'.

Not just a point of life or a piece of DNA but the coming together of those two pieces create the concept, in astral form, of a living something, whatever that something might be.

Then a further miraculous step follows.
Another piece of DNA is added that was actually created at the very beginning when the kindergarten part was going on.

This is a form of DNA that creates personality.

But this DNA was not placed in the hands of our God. It was put into the care of a special sort of angelic being who was tasked with carefully guarding this DNA until it was required.

So, once again the akashic record is called into play and every aspect of every sort of personality is stored in the akashic record.
Initially, this DNA is not directly connected to a person, animal, plant or mineral. It is just a stock of personality traits and are carefully guarded by a special sort of angelic being that was created long ago to keep all these personality traits in order and to distribute them when required.

Perhaps we could use the example of the quartermaster in a military camp who guards the various parts of military uniforms.
Initially, they do not belong to any particular soldier but, once distributed to the new recruits, it is they, the new recruits, to whom these items now belong.

It is a similar concept with personalities and we will explain this at greater length as it is both important and relevant to this book which attempts to describe personalities.

We break off for a moment to speak about personalities in relation to this book.

When we started this book we told you that we were going to take you into areas that had never been explored before and you may have wondered what we were going to describe. You may well have thought that we were going to explore an area of life totally strange to you.
And now we are saying that we are just going to tell you about personalities.

Personalities are not at all a new subject because all people have personalities and we know all about people and their different and sometimes strange personalities.

But you may have noticed that, in this book, we have already written a number of chapters and many thousands of words and still have not fully described personalities.

We crave your patience because the subject of personalities, the study of their origins and their uses is very complex and has never before been attempted even by the most respected psychotherapists and psychologists.

Generally speaking, they describe how people react to different personality traits and leave it at that.
We are tasked with explaining the origins of personality, how and why they were created and why we all have personalities - not the same thing at all and a difficult and complex subject to describe.

However, understanding personalities is an essential part of the spiritual growth of all of us, probably more than any of you could realise at the moment, so we ask you to read carefully this book because, as your life unfolds, both in incarnation and later in the spirit world, the understanding and, indeed, manipulation of personalities will be of paramount importance to you.

Therefore, please allow us to continue with this long and difficult task of describing how personalities are distributed, not only to people but, believe it or not, to all life wherever it is.
It may not be obvious at first glance to comprehend that everything has a distinct personality but, as all is one basically, if you have a personality all must have a personality to some degree.
It is only our personal development that blocks us from appreciating that everything must have some form of personality, from a grain of sand up to and including our entire multiverse.

Indeed, learning to feel and to respect the feelings of, just for example, mother Earth, is a sign of great spiritual advancement and of an advanced aspect of personality of the individual concerned.

Now, this is where we feel we should recapitulate somewhat what we have so far described in this book, and in others to a certain extent, and try to link it all together in as simple a fashion as possible because, unfortunately, the study of personalities is far from finished and we do not wish to pile new information on top of previously given information in an endless heap or both you and we will get lost in this maze.

Understanding personalities in medical areas is hard enough.
The average doctor has to complete his studies of the human body before he is permitted to delve into how medical people think the mind works so the average student doctor has to spend many years before he is considered to be qualified to try to help people with emotional problems.
Of course, you, once you have read and understood this book will know much more about the psychology of people than even the most qualified of doctors but we hope that you can appreciate that it will take us a great deal of study before we consider that we have given you enough information not only to understand who you are, but those of you who are interested in becoming healers will require all this information.

Much of it is new to man incarnate at the moment and we must also say that there are large numbers of people non incarnate who have never studied his complicated subject.

So we ask you to be patient and follow along as what we will reveal in this book will, eventually, be incorporated in medical studies thus helping student doctors to understand humanity.

Personality is of the greatest importance and a deep study of it is necessary in order to understand how life develops.

So, let us once again return to the basic development of life and then we can add other parts in a more understandable manner.

We mentioned that something called life was extracted from this singularity of life that was created by what we call God and that each aspect of life picked out by archangels was not only a tiny speck of life but was also the totality of life.

Perhaps, at the risk of losing your attention, we can spend a few lines to explain this.

This strange thing we call life is a force that exists. Quite where it came from we are not sure because the deeper we explore the origins of life, the more strange events we discover, each event based on the fact that life existed and each event requiring a manipulation of that life force.

We should, perhaps, inform you that, although we have given you information about life far in excess of any information previously given by any group, all this information is based on the fact that life already exists.
So all we can tell you at the moment is that, as far as our researchers have concluded, life has always existed.

The only real new information we can add is that life was not invented by our God but by, possibly, a greater being that we term the master creator.

We cannot even be sure that life was created by this master creator because, although he has created all the steps that enable life to develop as it has, at no point is there any indication that this wonderful master creator actually created life.
Indeed, much of his creation seems to be based on the assumption that life already existed and this master creator took basic life and built upon it to create all that we know and much more in areas that we have yet to discuss, for don't think for a moment that what we have so far told you is the limit of all that exists.
There are other areas of life yet to be discussed.
The only common denominator is that it is all based on life.

However, we have a singularity that we call God and this singularity is connected to all the Gods that we have so far mentioned, including our God and, we assume, the master creator.

So we want you to accept, if you will, that somewhere is an area that creates life in a singularity.

Quite where this life force is contained, we don't know.
As far as we are aware, the only beings that know where this life is kept are the archangels charged with selecting parts of it to create what is necessary to be created.
So, they reach into this singularity that we call life, but that we could also call consciousness, and take a portion which is not only a part but the totality of life.

To that they add a piece of DNA which tells that life force that it is going to be a something.
At that point it is placed in the eighth dimension of our planet.
So, in the eighth dimension, if we are just to consider you, you would be placed. At this point you would not know that you were going to be you because your identity had not yet been placed with you. You would just be life plus the knowledge that you were going to be a human.
One could almost compare it to an embryo in the womb of the mother of some type.
Life but no identity.

At some point, two people - who will become your parents - take the necessary steps and a foetus starts to grow in the womb of the lady who will become your mother.

So, the beings in the higher fourth dimension need to find someone who will be willing to incarnate in the family that now has a pregnant lady.
Obviously, this could be a lady anywhere in the world. A rich lady, a poor one. A lady in a developed country or a less developed one. You can work out the possibilities for yourself.

But all the possible choices are in the eighth dimension.
Further, they know that they are alive and they know that they are human. But that is all they know.

So a fairly large number of these embryo humans in the eighth dimension are invited down to the fourth dimension. And so a large number arrive.
We should perhaps say that we are referring to the upper fourth dimension in case there is any confusion.

Then a small portion of DNA which forms personality is placed with the potential humans.
There is just enough of this DNA to give the persons the desire to explore life.

So, they are placed in an over soul and what you might refer to as guides take them on conducted tours of all the areas of the heaven and hell that might interest them.

Now, we will mention at this point that we gave you impression that these young humans were being trained to incarnate in a particular family which would have only giving any young human the time of a gestation - nine months - to decide what he wants to be.
This was not true and we just used the story to illustrate what happens.

In fact, a young human might spend a long time exploring the heavenly realms before deciding what type of family he wants to be born in.

Therefore, do not assume that an embryo spiritual human is chosen to be born in a specific family at the same moment that a physical embryo is created in the womb of the physical mother.

A large number of non-physical human life forms are created and invited into the higher fourth dimension, given the necessary degree of life force and DNA to give it some degree of intelligence, placed in the care of an over soul and its education starts.

Then, as we have said, note is taken of each young human's interests and, eventually, it starts its journey through the personality galaxies.

So, we will end this chapter here and describe, in the next chapter, how all this happens with regard to the personality galaxies and, we hope, start to approach, at long last, how the master creator oversees all this.

CHAPTER 11

THE TWO PARTS OF PERSONALITY

So, in the last chapter we stressed the importance of a young spirit not only having a life force but also of sufficient DNA to tell it that it was a human and sufficient special DNA to give it some idea of what sort of human it wanted to be.

Before we go on to talk about the personality galaxies and the young human's path through them we mentioned a special sort of angel who guarded the DNA that was required when life was created, or should we say, required.
We mentioned that this special angel guarded the DNA connected to personality in the akashic record and issued it as and when required.

Once again, this angel is not visible to us.
It is far too advanced and holy so its vibrational frequency is far above ours which is why it is not visible to us.
But it is aware of each and every spirit, young or advanced, incarnate or non-incarnate and it issues or modifies personality amongst a few other things as required.
We don't know if you have picked up the mention of the word incarnate?
This implies that this angel is constantly surveying all life incarnate, including you, and alters the DNA connected to life and personality as required.

This implies that you, as you go through your incarnation and as you develop as a human and as your interests alter, have the DNA that is required for you to develop these interests given to you by this angel.
He monitors your interests, takes away those aspects of DNA that no longer interest you and replaces them in the akashic record and takes from the store DNA that corresponds to your new interests.
Then, as time passes and you start to age so you need modified DNA that corresponds not only to your aging body but the modified interests that you reject or develop.
Finally, at the moment of your demise from incarnation, this angel affects all the necessary changes required for you to acclimatize to life in the higher fourth dimension.

So this wonderful being is constantly in touch with all people, including you, and is monitoring your desires and changing interests (personality) and withdraws or replaces those aspects in the akashic record as required.

Now, we mentioned the word angel and an angel is usually imagined to be very much like a human and, indeed, there are angels like that but this angel is far removed from anything related to a human. It would be difficult to describe what he is because, by the very nature of the tasks he has to accomplish each and every moment, no human type of person could possibly do all this.

This angel is more like a machine. Not artificial intelligence we hasten to stress but an extremely complicated and powerful living force, rather like a warehouse that receives and issues parcels each day.

He is constantly surveying all life, everywhere: minerals, plants, animals and humans and is taking and replacing DNA in the akashic record as each entity requires change.

This also is new information never before revealed to people incarnate.

So, as this is new information we hope you will forgive us if we expand somewhat on this extraordinary being that we described as an angel and how it is able to be in active contact with all life, in all dimensions at the same time and able to comply with the desires, hopes and ambitions of all things simultaneously.

Logic would deny that such a thing were possible.
Can you imagine that anything that was alive: mineral, plant, animal and human either incarnate or discarnate could have each and every aspect of its personality constantly monitored and modified as the object concerned required?
And this endlessly throughout time!
Further, as even planets, galaxies, time and space are alive and thus have personalities, this being is monitoring these objects and/or events and are modifying them as life alters.

Once again, this seems like madness but we assure you is truth.

So, can we explain more fully what this angel is, where it is contained in the chain of life and any more about it that will make it seem to be a more plausible entity to you?

The first thing we must say that it is not in any way connected to humanity.
But it clearly must be, in some way, alive.

So this creates a problem. We have stated that everything created by God is alive. We will ignore all the various Gods and master creator and just say that by God we refer to a creative force.
So, anything made by a creative force must be alive.

Now, we know that minerals, plants, animals and humans are alive and we know that all the various angels and archangels are alive. But what sort of life force is this being that we have referred to, capable of monitoring and altering aspects of personality endlessly?

Clearly, by personality we refer to what are called the signs of the zodiac and we also said that for each aspect of personality there was a galaxy created under the control of a God.
But now we are saying that there is a being we called an angel stocking, storing and changing aspects of personality of all things as if there was some entity in charge of all the aspects of personality and controlling these personality galaxies and their Gods.

This is getting very complicated and we will need to explain all this very carefully or none of it will make sense.

Indeed, we wish that we did not have to explain this aspect of life to you because we said, at the very beginning of this book that we would be delving into areas of life never before explored.
We are now at that point and, reluctantly, we have been asked to explain all this to you.
But the problem is that there are only so many words in the English language and only so much that we can ask you to accept.

A number of times already we have stopped in the addition of new information and have recapitulated over and again what we have already explained.

We will not do so once more at this point except to ask you, if you are not sure of the way life is piled, piece by piece on top of itself, to go back to the beginning of this book and try to comprehend the layers.

So, we will go on from the point that we found ourselves, which was personality traits being brought forth or returned to memory banks in the akashic record.
Therefore, we ask you to accept that this life force we are dealing with is yet again a new form of life, in no way connected to life as we have previously described.
This may seem strange but as the various books we have yet to give you are written, we will have to explain that there are a large number of life forms that we have yet to reveal and explain to you.

The religious history of planet Earth tends to focus on one God and leads us to assume that that is all there is in creation.
Virtually all the information we have so far given you tends to reinforce this point of view. But, if you have read and understood what we have so far said in this book, we introduced you to the concept that there were other galaxies and other Gods that we said were related to personalities and even mentioned a super creator, a sort of developer of Gods.

Now we are asking you to believe in yet another sort of God or super God that is connected with the creation of personalities.
We mentioned that each personality galaxy had a God in charge of it, including our own galaxy, and now we are suggesting that, collectively, there is a master God that controls all the various Gods and galaxies that are related to personalities.

We could, of course, ask you to accept that just because there was a number of personality trends why should we consider that each one required a new galaxy and a new God?
Why could they not all just be functions of creation of life by our one exclusive God?

A fair question and one that we could easily accept, thus reducing the number of Gods required to one, as mentioned in our Bible and thus keeping life much more simple.

But the subject of personalities is not that simple.
We have found that personalities is a function of life in that nothing that is alive is so in a sterile form. Everything that is alive requires a form of intelligence, of awareness and that awareness we call personality.

Now, we do realise that words are beginning to fail us here. It is difficult enough to describe life and it is only the fact that you are alive and know that you are alive that enables us to get away with mentioning life without a long and difficult explanation. One would think that describing personality would be equally simple but, in fact, personalities are extremely difficult to describe, not because personalities are complicated but due to the origin of personalities and their place in the chain of life.

As we have said, personalities are a form of DNA and are stored in the akashic records. Also we said that there was a special kind of angelic being that was in charge of issuing or recuperating these pieces of DNA that correspond to personality.
But we have also said that there are galaxies, each one under the control of a God that corresponds to the basic forms of personality.
Lastly, we informed you that, before incarnation, you were placed in connection to the galaxy or galaxies that corresponded to who you were destined to be.
The same would apply to not only humans but to everything that exists.

We hope that you can begin to see how complex all this is becoming and it is the DNA that makes personalities that is responsible for all this complexity.

So we are gradually getting around to the idea that personalities are actually a form of DNA. This is, perhaps, not altogether as surprising as it might seem because even the police, when they examine DNA evidence from a crime scene are able to define a number of aspects of the person whose DNA is being examined.
For instance, examination can determine the sex, age and even race of the person concerned so it does not take too great a leap to realise that personality is connected to DNA.

But where does this lead us in relation to the orbs that we originally discovered in what we called an orb galaxy?
You may remember us describing a galaxy containing a large number of orbs that did not, at first glance, seem alive but later we realised did contain a form of life or at least of consciousness and that were under the control of a God.
Further, we conjectured that there were a large number of these galaxies, each one with its overseeing God and each Galaxy containing orbs, if not of living things, at least containing things that contained conscious objects.

Now, in order to advance this book we are going to ask you to accept that each one of these galaxies was there to promote a particular aspect of personality just as our galaxy promotes the aspect of love and just as our galaxy has a God to oversee that aspect of personality, so each one of these other galaxies has a God that oversees and promotes an aspect of personality.

But we told you that personalities are DNA and are stored in the akashic record.
So, have we not a problem here?

We have just said that personality is DNA and is stored in the akashic record under the control of an angel and now we are saying personality is a series of orbs contained in galaxies under the control of various Gods.
This sounds very much like a serious contradiction. How can we resolve this problem?

Once again we ask you to take a leap of faith with us and ask you to accept what we are going to explain because we do not have the facts at our disposal to back up our claims. This evidence will be revealed one day but is not yet available.
We can only describe events and leave you to accept or reject them.

What happens is this.

The DNA stored in the akashic record corresponds to personality. In fact we could say that DNA is personality, or the aspects we are talking about are.
DNA contains a huge number of different aspects and helps control a huge amount of different parts of us, some physical and some non-physical.
DNA is amazing.
It is deeply involved with virtually every aspect of life and, although it is not actually alive, we can say that it has awareness, a form of consciousness.

So, in the case of personality, we can say that the DNA that is stored in the akashic record is the end result of education given to it by the galaxy orbs.
By which we mean that for every type of personality aspect, angelic or archangelic beings calculate how many aspects of each personality are required. Then, that exact number of orbs are created, one for each person, animal, plant or mineral that will eventually require that type of personality.
We should say that each orb - which is a portion of that God - is given varying degrees of that personality aspect according to its need to have that aspect.

Then, once that is done, the orb is passed to the angel in charge of DNA and that orb is linked to a piece of DNA and it is placed in the akashic record.
This implies that the DNA of the orb and the DNA of the stored object is actually two pieces of DNA.

Now, we have explained this very important manner in which personality is created in a very quick and throwaway manner and we are sure that there are many of you that did not fully comprehend so please forgive us if we explain all this again in a more expanded fashion and at a more leisurely pace.

As you know, personality is very important and we all have one main personality trait and a number of lesser traits that go to make up who we are from a personality point of view.

Then we explained that personality is part of our DNA.
We also went on to say that the DNA that makes up our personality - each separate part of it - is actually divided into two parts. One part is the actual personality trait and the second part is the degree or intensity of that personality any person or object has.

It must be obvious that, as all is one, every object whether it is mineral, animal, vegetable or human must have the same emotions or personality. But it must also be obvious that a grain of sand does not require any personality trait to be present or developed to the same degree that many humans have.
For instance, we imagine that a stone would not have the same emotion of love, or indeed, hate developed where as we know that humans are capable of extremes of these two emotions.

So this is where the two parts of personality come in.
One part gives all life the concept of all the possible personality aspects as a concept and the second part tells the personality aspect what degree of intensity of those emotions are required.

To repeat, if we may, just to clarify the point.
Everything, no matter what it is has all the personality aspects present but each individual object or being has these personality aspects present in varying degrees according to the type of object they might be and according to the depth of development that any object might have.

So, as we have said before, a stone requires a less developed personality than a plant and a plant requires less than some animals.
But, for instance, some animals are capable of projecting love more than others.
At the top of the tree, of course, is man who is capable of demonstrating extremes of emotion.

So, emotions or personalities are in two parts: the basic personality concepts and the personal degree of development of these personality traits.
All this is then stocked in the akashic record.

However, there is much more to the story than what we have so far mentioned.

We must go on to delve into the way the personality traits are connected to our auras and how our auras affect us in our daily lives, no matter what dimension we happen to live in.

There are also other aspects that we must touch on because personality is an essential part of our make-up and, if it were not for personalities, we would all be like robots.

So, we will end this chapter here and turn our attention to other aspects of personality.

CHAPTER 12

THE HOLY SPIRIT

So, to add to the confusion concerning personalities we must now turn our attention to the way that what we have so far links to a different part of humanity.
We refer to the parts of the God life spirit that joins with the DNA involved with personality.

This sounds like the usual gobbledygook so let us go a long way back in the books we gave you to explain.

At one stage we mention that the God spirit, that ultimately links with the Higher Self, nevertheless also links with the part of us that is generally ignored but is actually a staging post between the God spirit and the rest of us.
It is possible that you do not remember us mentioning this part of the chain or that you have never seen or read the explanation.

This is a part that is often confused with the life spirit itself and, in the phrase, 'the Father, the Son and the Holy Spirit' it is the part that is the Holy Spirit.

So we have the Father, which is God itself and the Holy Spirit which, despite any other connotation that various sectors of Christianity might put to it, actually refers to the staging post between God and the Higher Self (the Son).

We do not wish to get into a theological or religious argument about whatever meaning any reader of this book might put into the three terms we mentioned. The part of the phrase that interests us is the third part - the Holy Spirit.
So please accept, if you can, our interpretation of the three terms.
In our interpretation, Father equates to God, Son equates to Higher Self and the Holy Spirit is the part in between God and the Higher Self.

The problem is that the Higher Self is part of the fifth dimension. As we have told you, there is only one Higher Self for all life.
But we have also explained that, depending on the degree of sentience, so whatever object is being considered, the degree of sentence can vary widely, a stone being less sentient then a human or, indeed, an angel.

This is where all the personality stuff that we have gone to great lengths to explain comes in to help divide sentence according to the requirements of the various objects: animal, vegetable, mineral or human.
So, we have done our best to help you to understand that personality is basically DNA and, despite being spread over a fairly wide area of consciousness, is ultimately stored in the akashic record. We have also said that the akashic record is actually another term for the Higher Self. So akashic record and Higher Self are the same thing.

We have also said that personalities are created from DNA.
Thus, at least part of the akashic record and part of the Higher Self are capable of handling DNA.
As we progress through these books we will discover that virtually everything to do with life is connected to DNA in one way or another.

But the Higher Self is not DNA.
The akashic record is largely DNA but the Higher Self is not although it is capable of accepting and handling DNA.

This makes another complication because we said that the akashic record is virtually all DNA but that the Higher Self, despite being the same as the akashic record, is not made of DNA.
Therefore, for the Higher Self to be able to accept DNA, a sort of transformer is required.

Strange as this may seem, this is where the Holy Spirit comes in.
The Holy Spirit is pure spirit and, like God, is not contained in any dimension.
But something is necessary that is capable of accepting information that is of a purely spiritual nature but, at the same time, is capable of accepting information that is DNA based.
The Holy Spirit is that transformer.

We repeat once more that personality is of extreme importance in the construction of life and the more sentient an object is, the greater role that personality plays in the construction of that object.
By object, of course, we refer to anything alive; animal, vegetable or mineral.
As humans are the most advanced of God's creatures - if we ignore angels etc., - we will just concentrate on the way the Holy Spirit acts in regard to humans.

You will have noticed that we placed the Holy Spirit next to God, the creative force, which gives some idea of the importance that personality and DNA has in the construction of life in general and man in particular.

So, we need to try to understand something about the Holy Spirit.

We have said that it is a spiritual force and thus is not contained in any one of the auras or dimensions.
DNA, even the very high sort that we have been describing, could be considered as physical in that it has a sort of practical aspect to it as opposed to being pure spirit. The Holy Spirit is a spiritual force but, at the same time, it is capable of dealing with DNA.
This is why we call it a transformer.
This is perhaps not the most accurate term we could have used but we wish to imply that the Holy Spirit is a force that can take one thing and link it to another.
Also, it can do this in both directions, by which we mean that the Holy Spirit can take a purely spiritual concept and transform it into DNA, which has a sort of physicality to it, and/or take DNA and transform it into a spiritual force.

Now, this is opening the door into looking at personality in a new and different way,

We are going to ask you to accept slightly new and different ways of considering a few words because there are some concepts for which words do not exist.

In the case of DNA, although this very high sort that we are considering in this book is not at all physical in the sense that we normally ascribe to the meaning, we are going to ask you to allow us to use the word 'physical' when we mention this high form of DNA as opposed to a truly spiritual force such as God.
We hope this is clear but we will repeat.
When we mention DNA, we ask you to think of it as physical but when we use the term spiritual we are considering a force that has no concept of physical.

Thus, when mentioning the Holy Spirit, we want you to consider it to act in two ways, the first being spiritual and the second physical. That is why we called it a transformer.
It may seem bizarre to think of the Holy Spirit as being in any way connected to personality but it is so.

Until now, when talking about personality, we have tended to mention more or less exclusively DNA, which we described as physical and avoided any mention of a spiritual connotation.
We did this deliberately as personality is extremely complicated and we did not wish to jumble the DNA aspect of it with any connection to God but that connection exists and we must now address that connection.

To be honest, if we think of personality and if we think of all the huge mass of life, it should be obvious that the creative force - God, if you will - should play a role somewhere. If you think back to the beginning of this book and if you consider what we have explained, chapter by chapter, it should be clear that personality is not only extremely complicated but must surely be linked back to the creative force (God) somehow.

So we are going to try to explain how the spiritual aspect of personality, using our terms, links to the physical, to create a more comprehensive understanding of what personality truly is.
Perhaps we should say that there are other facets that we will broach later but the spiritual aspect must be dealt with, which is what we are going to attempt to do it now.

Thus, this chapter will deal with the way in which the God force is connected to personality.
Once again, we inform you that this is information that will be new to you as it has never before been explained in quite this fashion.

In order to make what we wish to say to you understandable, we need to go back to the beginning of our explanation of what God is in relation to humanity. We will ignore all other life forms for the sake, not only of verbal economy, but also in order not to get lost in confusion. Thus, we will consider just humanity although we know that you will be able to accept that what we say about man will apply to all life.

God, as we have said, creates life. That is all that God does.
In fact, if you have followed our teachings you will know that God created just one life.
But, and this is where the Holy Spirit starts to come in, God created what we have previously termed awareness or consciousness.
This was able to create the idea that there were a large number of creations.
We mentioned the ID which is something that allows you to think of yourself as an independent living object.
If you advance enough spiritually, you may reach the point where you can appreciate your oneness to all life but your ID is constantly informing you that you are you, an independent life force separate and remote from any other lifeforce, human or anything else.

So we need to find which part of us provides us with the knowledge that we are an independent life force.
In other words, we need to find, to locate, the source of the ID. Not only do we need to locate where the ID is but we need to know why it exists and all that we can find out about it including if it is physical or spiritual.

Now, it may not surprise you that the ID is connected to personality which, itself, is connected to DNA.
Therefore, we could consider the ID to be linked to our meaning of the word physical.
But we also link personality to spiritual in that personality comes from the fact that God (a spiritual force) created not only one life force but also created the concept of multiple life forces.

This is starting to get complicated again so let us try to explain it in simple terms.

Life is created by God. But God only created one life force. However, God required more from life than just one life force so the concept of multiple life forces was introduced.
This concept is spiritual.
However, as we move into accepting multiple life forces we start to call that the ID. But we tend to link the ID to DNA.
At some point we need to create a change, a link from a spiritual force to a physical force. Or we could say that is just a change from pure spirit to DNA.
However we look at it, we need to transform pure God construction to physical DNA and also link it all to personality.
This is where the Holy Spirit comes in.

The Holy Spirit accepts the one God force into one side of it and then splits it into a myriad of separate parts and gives each new part of the concept of the ID, which is the way that all things think of themselves as independent life forms.
This ID, which is DNA, can thus link itself to personality.

Let us repeat this to make sure that it is quite clear.

God created life. But God only created one life.
Realising that this one life was not satisfactory, God's Archangels, implementing God's desire, needed to find a way in which this one life form could be persuaded to think of itself as countless lifeforms.

First, the concept of DNA was created and then a form of personality was brought into existence.
This form of personality is called an ID.
There is actually only one ID for all life but the magic is that, through personality, all life thinks it has a unique access to the ID in a personal sense.
This is achieved by altering the spiritual force of the creation of the one life force to the spiritual force of the one ID and then changing it into DNA which allows it to think of itself as multiple life forces.

We do realise that we have not explain this very clearly but it is not easy to find words to describe taking one thing and, by changing it from spiritual to physical, creating the idea that, from this one life force, countless life forces can be imagined.
Anyway, this is the task that the Holy Spirit accomplishes.
The Holy Spirit takes the one spiritual life force and transforms it into a multitude of physical entities.

The editor of this book asked Great White Brotherhood if they would clarify further their understanding of the ID. These few lines, written in italics, were what the editor was told.
"The ID is, at its base, a spiritual manifestation. That is why there is only one.
So, if we consider the major spiritual aspects which, being just one of each, are not connected to physicality, we have three.
1. The God spirit itself.
2. The Higher Self.
3. The Holy Spirit.
Now, the ID is more difficult to place as it is both spiritual and DNA (physical).
It is not contained within any of the auras whilst it is in its solo spiritual form but is when it is used by life to help create personality.
Thus, in what we might term its physical form (helping create independence), part of it can be found in the sixth dimension.
So, it is, in a way, on either side of the Higher Self. In spiritual form it is close to the Holy Spirit but in its DNA form it can be found close to personality. Then it is on the physical side of the Higher Self."

We must admit that what we have described is not the exact truth because there are other aspects to the Holy Spirit that it would, at the moment, be inappropriate to mention. It would just cause confusion but we do not like to hide truth from you so, if we can, at some point in this book, finding an opening to describe more of the Holy Spirit, we will. For the moment, please accept the explanation we have provided.
It is complicated enough we think you will agree without piling more on top.

We have not yet finished explaining the transformer function of the Holy Spirit.

The question, amongst others, is how the Holy Spirit can take a spiritual force and transform it into what we term a physical force. Or, to put it in other words, to take a spiritual, Godly force and change it into DNA.
As always, there is an easy answer and a complicated one.

The easy answer is that something we call consciousness, or that we call the ID, takes the one spiritual life spirit and, by connecting it to the ID, which thinks that it is multiple beings. As the ID is connected to DNA, the transformer merely does its job which is to change one into many and the trick is performed.
Obviously, this is not the whole answer because we need to explain what this 'trick' is, that we also called magic, although, as you should know by now, there is no such thing as magic. It is all just advanced physics.

Any of you who have even basic knowledge of electronics will know that a transformer can take one voltage and change it into another.
Equally, on one side of a transformer, we can measure a single voltage and on the other we can measure multiple taps of different voltages.
Also, from a transformer it is possible to take alternating current (AC) and, with the help of a circuit, convert it to direct current (DC).
So we are used to having transformers converting electricity according to the needs and desires of the circuit designer. Real life is often not too different to life as we live it.

Let us use our imaginations somewhat and try to use the electric or electronic transformer concept and see how it equates to real life.

We start off on one side of the Holy Spirit with the one, pure spirit, God force.
Now, the God force is vibration (frequency) that we could call AC.
Obviously, we are using an analogy to say this but, at the same time, it is not that far from the truth as an electric circuit feeds AC current into one side of a transformer and the one God force is also an AC power.
Then, with a normal transformer, this one AC current can be changed in a number of ways, either higher or lower voltages or multiple voltages.

In the case of the Holy Spirit, very much the same thing occurs. This one God force is converted into a huge number of taps, according to the number of animal, vegetable, mineral or human entities that exist, including time, space, planets, galaxies, gravity and every conceivable thing that has been created in our reality. We should perhaps say that we would need to include alternate realities and all the beings that live in them in this calculation.
So, this would make a truly stupendous number of secondary taps on the second side of the transformer we call the Holy Spirit, but God is not limited by such matters.

Thus, we now have at our disposition - or rather, God's archangels have - this incalculable number of frequencies, as we have described above. This opens the way for just one life force (God) to appear to be multiple life sources.

However, electric or electronic circuits with which we are familiar are not very useful in creating TVs, amplifiers, computers etc., just using AC electricity.
Many of them tend to require the AC current on the secondary tap(s) to be converted into DC before they can be used to create electronic devices.
The reason for this does not concern us at the moment but we will go on comparing God's created life to electronic circuits, if we may, for a bit longer.

Electronic circuits often require a circuit that converts AC current into DC.

Now, God does not require this exactly but there is, attached to the secondary taps of the Holy Spirit, a circuit that changes the AC that came from the secondary taps of the Holy Spirit transformer into DNA.

This circuit, obviously, does not exist in any way that would be understood like one might understand a DC converter.
This circuit is another form of DNA.
DNA can take many forms and, especially when we are dealing with personality, there seems to be almost no limit to the varieties of DNA that are employed.

You may remember us mentioning the akashic record made of DNA, the ID containing DNA, the orbs being made of DNA and a number of other things we mentioned either in this book or others, especially the book about DNA. We wish you to understand that all, or most, DNA mentioned is unique.
It is all different according to its ultimate use.

So, the DNA that converts AC frequency from the God force to DNA that can be used to create all that God requires to generate sentient life, can be considered as an AC/DC converter used in electronic circuits.

Now, we don't want to stretch this analogy of comparing electronic circuits to the way the God force is altered in DNA, which can be used by life, too far.
However, we are grateful that electronic circuits exist because it does give us an easily understandable example to explain how the one God force (pure vibration) is converted into all the DNA that life requires.

We are going to use the analogy of electronic circuits one more time as there exists an example that, with a stretch of the imagination, can equate to life.

We will mention electronic valves (tubes) that used to be used before what are called solid state devices were invented.

We may use valves (tubes) as an example as they utilities three different sorts of electricity and, in a way, life does too.
From the secondary, or output, of the transformer, DC is generated which equates to DNA.
Also, AC is generated which is used to power the heater circuit in a valve (tube).
In real life, God's AC power is present in various strengths to give the ID, amongst other things, the sense of oneness to God.
Then, lastly, there is the AC signal, whatever it needs to be, which, just in the case of a musical instrument, takes the weak signal from that instrument and amplifiers it.
In the case of life, this AC God force is what we call life.
This is the force that gives all things created by God independent life.

However, we have used this analogy enough and we do not wish to wear it out!
Also, we understand that there may be many that do not understand anything about electronics and even fewer who know how valves (tubes) function.
But we needed to find something that we could use as an example of how the Holy Spirit functions and that was the best that we could find.
For those with no knowledge of electronics, we ask you to forgive us and we hope that you have managed to follow how the Holy Spirit works anyway.

We must also say that what we explained was by way of simple analogy and that, in reality, the Holy Spirit does not act exactly in the way a transformer does, although the comparison is close enough that we feel comfortable using it.

The next problem is that, linked to the output of the Holy Spirit are a vast number of connections, mostly DNA, that combine to create living creatures, including humans.
If we tried to describe all these links, it would require a book in its own right and we wanted to limit this part of the explanation about personality to just one chapter.
We think that what we described so far concerning the Holy Spirit is complicated enough without giving a complete picture.

This applies to most things concerning life. There are so many facets to life that to describe all of it would need an immense encyclopedia.

We wish you to have a comprehensive understanding of life but there is a limit to what we can describe.

We have tried to describe how personality works from a number of different directions. This latest one, connected to the Holy Spirit, is one of the most unexpected but we assure you that it is a vital aspect. Without the Holy Spirit acting as a transformer, changing the one God spirit into a multitude of different components, many of them connected to DNA and the God power transformed in frequency and power, personality would not exist and without personality life as we know it could not exist.

So we end this rather complicated chapter here and turn to the auric fields or dimensions.

CHAPTER 13

THE UPPER 4TH DIMENSION

In the last chapter we looked at the way the God force was able, via the Holy Spirit, to create the impression that there are countless individual entities.
This is in part due to the fact that everything is living in a world of illusion.
Even though what we call the plane of imagination is the 6th dimension, nevertheless, due to the fact that no matter in which dimension life lives it is all created from and, in fact is, just one force - God - so, in a way, all the dimensions contain fiction.
This, obviously, needs to be explained.

In reality, various dimensions are real as they were created by God but any life that they might contain is the result of what was created via the Holy Spirit as we explained in the last chapter and so is, to use the word, imaginary.
Not just the beings in the 6th dimension but all life no matter in which dimension it is to be found.

We do not like to use the word imaginary as it is not exactly true but there is not a word in the English language to describe exactly what life is.

If you have read and understood chapter twelve, you will know that from the one spiritual God force, thanks to the Holy Spirit, DNA and personality, this one force thinks that it is everything.
So, this must be illusion but it is illusion created from one reality - God. Thus, we have two realities in one. We have the God force from which all entities are created and then we have the entities themselves which are imaginary but, thanks to DNA and personality, seem to be totally real.

So, for there to be one word that would encapsulate all that we would need a word that explains two states; one real and one imaginary or created. Such a word does not exist.
But it is important that the student of esoteric matters understands clearly that he/ she/ it is living in two states simultaneously.
The first being the one unique God force and the second this created illusion.

In another chapter we mentioned that there were other galaxies and other Gods and that they, too, contributed to the creation of personality.
Once again, these galaxies are distantly connected to our galaxy as they help create personalities so they are creating illusions also although the Gods in charge of these galaxies are real.

Lastly, we mention the master creator which, obviously, is real.

We will just mentioned that this is not the end of creation as there are other areas to explore but that must wait for other books as any description of other realities - truly real or imaginary - must wait until we come to the books we intend to give you.
We are exploring personality at the moment and we think that you will find this difficult enough to comprehend without worrying about yet other matters.
We merely mentioned this to help sow the seeds of a pigeon hole in your mind in which, eventually, to store more information.

This chapter, as we said, is about how the auras relate to personality.

Now, we have mentioned auras or dimensions before many times and have given you a book about them - auras and dimensions being two words to describe the same thing. We tend to use the word aura when describing how they interact with life and dimension when describing the nuts and bolts of them, if you will forgive the expression.

We do not intend to explain in any great detail the auras as we have given you an entire book and if you are not sure what auras or dimensions are, please read the book on auras.

However, as we unfold this chapter we will mention that dimensions 1, 2 and 3 do not concern us, dimensions 1 and 2 containing hate-filled creatures, even though they are illusionary. But we prefer not to mention them if and when we can.
Dimensions 3 is empty for the moment so there is nothing to talk about in that dimension. It may be that God has future plans for that dimension but, for the moment, it is not used. So this chapter will limit itself to dimensions 4 to 8 and then only in as far as they concern the construction of personalities.

So, let us try to explain one more time these various dimensions and how life as we imagine it to be and as we visualise it is placed in them.

The problem is, of course, that having giving you a complete book on the subject of dimensions and, indeed, life as they are placed in them (life in plural), it should be possible to link it all together without our help. But we are considering personalities and they are linked to DNA so we will consider how life links to DNA and thus to personalities from this point of view which presents a new aspect of understanding life.

Let us take the top 2 dimensions referred to as 8 and 7.

Perhaps, if we repeat ourselves somewhat you will forgive us because we must consider the many people who have not studied the information we have given you on dimensions or auras (the same thing), so to make sure we are all on the same page we will need to explain a few things once again.

Perhaps we should say to start off that there are 8 dimensions.
Despite these 8 dimensions being split into countless sub dimensions, each sub dimension created to house an aspect of life, nevertheless, there are just 8 basic dimensions.

Next, in order to try to explain the way life unfolds in, on and around these dimensions, none of them have any more spiritual importance than any other.

We know that there are people who create fantasy concerning dimensions and create the most fantastic nonsense concerning them.
The first is to say that there are more than 8 dimensions.
We have heard people claim to have spirit guides from ever higher dimensions, far in excess then the 8 that actually exist and give the impression that the higher the number of a dimension the more holy it is.
Thus, we have heard people state that their guide is from a ridiculously high level that is just below God itself. Indeed, we have heard people claim that their guide is God.
Equally, if not God, it might be Jesus, Saint this or Saint that.
Now, we do not like to criticize anyone but we would suggest that if you come across any information created by anyone pretending to be channeling a guide from some very high dimension or from God, Jesus etc., you treat that person and their information with the greatest circumspection.

There are 8 dimensions and, although each one serves a unique function, none of them are any more holy than any other.
The dimensions are just bands of frequency created by God to allow life to unfold and expand.
They are not in any way connected to higher and higher levels of holiness.

This is not to say that there are not levels of higher or lower holiness but they are not spread out across an immense number of dimensions.

You will find when you get there that the vast majority of holy or unholy people - Saints or Devils, if you will - are housed in the 4th dimension with links to the 5th and 6th dimensions (which we will explain later although we have already explained this before).

The degree of holiness or unholiness is connected to higher or lower personal frequencies within the 4th dimension. Once again, we have explained all this and have linked it all to the law of mutual attraction.

But life as we know it to be starts off in the 8th dimension at which point aspects of God are placed there just as points of life without any denomination. This denomination will at some point be given by God's archangels placing a logos with them that tells them what they are going to be; animal, vegetable or mineral.
This logos is actually DNA and the origin of that DNA can be traced back to the Holy Spirit as we explained in this book.
Once a point of life has this logos with it, it knows what it is going to be and it then moves down to the 7th dimension to develop somewhat according to its destination.
But let us just consider humans and just as far as it concerns personality.

A human obviously requires a lot more treatment than a life spirit destined to become a grain of sand or a raindrop but, as all is one, so they all follow the same course.

It is the degree of education that varies according to the needs of each object to have advanced knowledge or not.
This advanced knowledge is provided in the form of DNA. A human or a grain of sand follow the same course but the type of DNA that a grain of sand is given is much different than that given to a human.
There are a large number of different sorts of DNA and they are under the control of the angel we mentioned and are stored in the akashic record until required to be distributed to the life aspects.

The DNA, stored in the akashic record, is in the 5th dimension.
The 5th dimension, amongst other things, contains the akashic record and it also contains the Higher Self.
So, life in general and humans in particular are given links to the 5th dimension from which it can do a number of things.
The God spirit itself is connected to the embryo human via the 5th dimension and the DNA that helps form the spirit is also contained in the 5th dimension.

Now, this next bit might seem a bit complicated.

We said that life, once given a logos, was placed in the 7th dimension.
But we mentioned that DNA was in the 5th dimension.
We gave the impression that DNA was extracted from the akashic record in the 5th dimension and given to the embryo spirit in the 7th dimension.
This is both true and not true.
It is true that DNA is attached to the spirit in the 7th dimension but it is not removed from the 5th dimension.
Although the spirit in the 7th dimension is able to use the DNA attached to it, nevertheless the DNA actually remains within the akashic record in the 5th dimension.

Thus we can say that, at all times, humans and all life are permanently connected to the akashic record and can have access to it when required.
As a person develops and as his interests and life experiences change so he can release DNA and link with new DNA.
He also has a similar connection to the Higher Self.
The Higher Self remains in the 5th dimension while the embryo spirit remains in the 7th dimension.

Further, in the case of the Higher Self, there is only one but obviously there are countless life spirits so it is only through independent frequencies that form a connection between the life spirit and the Higher Self that enable the embryo spirit and the Higher Self to have a permanent link.

Then, of course, we move onto the 6th dimension which is the one, amongst many things, that deals with imagination.
Once again, the young spirit remains in the 7th dimension but has a permanent link to what is going on in the sixth dimension.

So, to make this quite clear, undeveloped spirits of life are stocked in the 8th dimension.
Once they have been chosen to be something they move to the 7th dimension.
It is at this point that they start reacting with DNA and start to become more recognisable as "something" whatever that something might be.
It is also at this point that, through DNA, personality starts to form.

It might be possible for a grain of sand or a raindrop to live without much personality, but in the case of a human, if they did not all have distinct personalities they would be very strange humans indeed.
The personality is DNA as we have explained.

Finally, it is usually required that the life spirits of all types move to the upper 4th dimension.
Once again, we remind you that virtually everything, if it is going to go to an incarnation, will move to the upper 4th dimension
You may know this as the Heavenly sphere but it is much more than that.
It is about the busiest dimension of all.

Most people that know about the 4th dimension only know of the Heavenly spheres but there is an enormous amount more going on than just Heaven.

So, although we said that this chapter would just consider how dimensions and personality are linked we will take the opportunity of expanding somewhat on this dimension, especially as much of it concerns personalities and their associated DNA.

We must first say that the 4th dimension is divided into two parts, the higher and the lower.
If you have followed the wisdom we have shared with you, you will know this.
The higher 4th being the area of positivity and the lower negativity. Both areas are equally important and both areas contain life forces in similar numbers and shades of development.
Obviously, the DNA that forms their personalities and thus their actions is vastly different but all life follows the same pattern and thus the DNA that is issued to lifeforms, either in the higher 4th or the lower is stored in the akashic record. All is one, we remind you.

But let us first consider the higher 4th before moving on to consider the lower, although, once you have understood what is occurring in the higher 4th dimension you will easily understand activities occurring in the lower 4th as they are very similar.

But our interest for the moment is to try to describe what occurs in the higher or upper 4th part.
We must first say that what separates the upper from the lower is frequency (vibration).
The 4th dimension, like all dimensions, has a basic carrier wave but within that carrier wave are a vast number of sub frequencies - one for each living object that is found there.

So, the sub frequencies start off at a certain vibration and rise in frequency until there are sufficient sub frequencies to allow each living objective being to be housed.
By which we mean that each and every entity, whether he be positive or negative, has the same basic frequency as his sub frequency carrier wave which allows him to maintain his connection to a sub frequency within the 4th dimension.

We wish also to say that each entity, whether he be Saint or Demon, is alive and has the God logos with him just as you have. All is one.

So, everything that is in the 4th dimension started out as a point of life in the 8th dimension, was selected by archangels and given the DNA that told it what it was destined to become. Understanding this fact has startling consequences.

As we have often said, you were, at one point long ago, just a point of life in the 8th dimension but, by chance, were selected to become a human and you were given the logos, which is actually a sort of DNA, that made you into a human.
But before you were given that stamp, that logos, that DNA, you were just a point of life created by God and you could have become anything.
Indeed, you could have not been selected at all and thus could still be a point of life in the 8th dimension.

Thus, we wish you to understand that when negative creatures were required the archangels could have selected any point of life in the 8th dimension but just selected the number of points of life required to fulfill the need for positive or negative creatures, gave them the necessary DNA and move them to the 7th dimension.
It is important to understand that negative creatures are not much different from you or any of us. We all started out in the 8th dimension, were selected to be something and then moved to the 7th dimension.

So, although demons, djinns etc., are dangerous and best left alone, they follow the same path that you did and still do. The only difference is the DNA that was given to them.
The DNA that you were given created a human and, generally, humans are positive people. Demons are exactly the same except that the DNA they were given told them that they were part of the negative forces and thus, in the 7th dimension, they were pushed down a different educational path to humans.

But when all life had completed its education and had been given all the DNA that it needed to form its personality it was taken to the 4th dimension and put in the care of an oversoul where it would receive further education if necessary.
So, demons and all negative beings, due to something called the law of mutual attraction, are drawn to the part of the 4th dimension commensurate to their frequency.

In case you have not understood this part, let us expand as it is quite interesting.
Everything is basically the same and largely follows the same path but also, obviously, a raindrop, for instance, does not require the same education as a human.

As education proceeds, different sorts of DNA are given to it to teach it to perform its function well so a raindrop, a grain of sand and a human all receive education, are given the DNA they require to fulfill the functions that they are destined for and also their basic vibration alters. Some have higher frequencies and some lower depending on what they are to become and thus the DNA they are given.

We wish to say something about water that should be obvious but that very few people realise. The same applies to minerals but we will consider just water.

The archangels today almost never need to create more water.
Long years ago, when the illusionary world in which you live was created, a certain amount of water was also created.
The strange thing is that exactly the same amount of water is on Earth today as was created when planet Earth was created.
Planet Earth has a cover over it sometimes called the Firmament that seals the planet in a shield of gravity.
This prevents any water from disappearing.
No matter where water is, in clouds, rivers, lakes, seas, in the Earth or in underground caverns, no matter what you do to water, like boiling it, it reforms and remains exactly the same amount as when the planet was created.
So, the archangels almost never need to worry about creating more water.
It is all in the sixth dimension, the world of illusion in which you all live, and there it remains.

The same applies to minerals.

Thus, although water and minerals are just as alive as you, they do not need as much attention as you do.
We will just say that as Ascension proceeds, water and minerals will slightly change and increase in frequency as planet Earth increases in frequency but for the moment the change is very slow and so not much attention to them is required.
Other, more alive objects; plants, animals and humans obviously require more attention and thus occupy the archangels and the directors of life more - especially humans.

We were talking about the upper 4th dimension and got sidetracked. Let us return to the upper 4th.

As you know, the upper 4th dimension is the place you return to when your incarnation is finished.
Regardless of the life you lived on Earth, holy, middling (or ordinary) or evil, you will spend the rest of your life - which will be to all intents and purposes infinite - in the upper 4th.

There is a lot of confusion about what is called hell.
Most people think that it is a totally separate place from heaven and many think that unless you are a devout Christian, no matter how good and kind of person you were

during your incarnation, unless you were a Christian, God will condemn you to suffer in hell for all eternity.
There are other religions that purport the same thing.
In fact, nothing could be further from the truth.

The problem is that explaining heaven and hell is not easy because words often fail us. We have explained the connection of heaven to hell many times but will do so once again as where a person ends up once his incarnation is finished is connected to his personality. So, we will explain once again.

If you have understood what we have told you in this book and other knowledge we have shared with you, you will know that everything is vibration.
So, each person has a basic vibration or frequency.

People also have free will and, as they went through the long educational process before incarnation, they were presented with lots of experiences and were able to choose which things they were attracted to.

With regards to the aspects of personality connected to kindness or unkindness, the ability to put others first or not, the desire to create peace or not and so on, people draw towards them these aspects of personality.

This is a natural process and the teachers take note of their pupil's preferences but do not try to persuade the pupil to move in any direction. The pupil has free will.
But, according to the personality that the pupils develop they draw from the DNA in the akashic record the type of DNA that helps them develop a particular type of personality.
So, if we simplify things, people tend to be either very kind, very hurtful, or just ordinary people.

Thus, the people vibrate at particular frequencies.
The hurtful people vibrate at a low frequency, the ordinary people vibrate at a higher frequency and the very nice people vibrate at a yet higher frequency.

Obviously, this is a simplification. In reality, there are a huge number of personality types but the same rules apply. If one is a nasty person he vibrates at a low frequency, if he is kinder, his vibration is higher and very nice people vibrate with a yet higher frequency. All these frequencies are connected to the type of person one chooses to be and are created through the personality trend provided by the DNA that he draws to him.

We hope that you have understood this. It is not complicated but has great consequences once one's incarnation is finished and the person returns home to the upper 4th dimension.

Let us now look at heaven and hell.
Contrary to what people think both heaven and hell are an integral part of the same portion of heaven.

They are separated by vibration.
So, what are referred to as heaven and hell occupy the same portion of the upper 4th dimension but contain a vast number of frequencies which will correspond to the frequencies of people. People that vibrate to a low frequency will be naturally drawn to a part of heaven or hell that matches their frequency while people that vibrate to a higher frequency will be drawn to a part that matches their frequency.
It is all quite simple and is all a natural event caused by the law of mutual attraction.

We will explain this again to make it quite clear.

In a certain portion of the upper or higher 4th dimension Is an area that is called heaven and/or hell.
We will say that we do not refer to it in those terms but what we call it is of no importance.
What is important for you to understand is that there is an area that is used to separate people according to their level of spirituality. But it is all one place.

It is not, as many people think, two separate areas, heaven and hell. It is all one huge area.
Within that area are an enormous number of sub frequencies and each one of these sub frequencies contains landscapes of vibrations commensurate to the sub frequencies of each sub dimension.

That might be difficult to understand so let us explain again.

The heaven/hell area contains a huge number of landscapes that correspond to the frequency of that sub dimension.
You could imagine it as a number of countries each one formed with different landscapes.
So, some contain beautiful garden areas with lawns, lakes, rivers, flower beds and so on. Some contain barren wastelands and some look rather like we imagine the moon to look. Equally, in some areas there is bright sunshine and it is warm and in others there is little light and it is cold and bleak.
There are many, many such areas each one separate from the others and each one vibrating at a certain frequency from low to high.
The dark, bleak, dismal areas we call hell and the bright, beautiful areas we call heaven.

If we consider vibrations (frequencies) from the lowest to the highest, they create these landscapes so the lowest are unpleasant indeed but, as the frequencies rise, so the landscapes become nicer until we arrive at areas so bright and beautiful that we couldn't really describe them.

The bleak ones we call hell and the bright ones heaven.

Now, and this is the important part, each one of these many areas corresponds approximately to the frequency of each person incarnate.

When a person's incarnation is finished, his body is disposed of but all that is immortal; spirit, soul and all the personality aspects, amongst others, is transferred not only to the higher 4th dimension but that part that we call heaven/hell.

He arrives, first, at a sort of halfway place that is referred to as Summerland.

He arrives at this halfway place despite how evil he might be or how holy he might be. He is shown around Summerland to give him time to acclimatise to his new life.

Eventually, he is shown the life he led on earth during his incarnation. His life review. At this point he has the opportunity to repent for any harm he caused. If he repents, this has the effect of raising his vibrational rate. If he does not repent his frequency remains much as it was. If he is glad for the harm he caused, his frequency lowers further.

So you can see that no one can accuse anybody of judging them.
First and foremost, the life that the person lead on Earth forms his personality.
Actually, it would be better to say that his personality was formed in the higher 4th dimension whilst he was being shown around that area before incarnating.
He had the opportunity to be drawn towards holy things or unholy things. The person chooses for himself. No one tries to push him in any direction.

Eventually, he faces incarnation and, once again, he chooses in which direction to develop.
By the law of mutual attraction he is drawn towards following a kind path or an unkind path but the person may change at any moment.
His life plan will guide him according to the choices he made before incarnation but he may alter his life plan if he really wants to in relation to being kind or unkind.
But, sooner or later his incarnation ends and he arrives in Summerland.
Eventually, he sees his life on Earth - his life review - not only from his point of view but also from the point of view of those with whom he interacted.

It must be said that no one is perfect. By the very nature of incarnation, we are constantly interacting with others. The life spirit (God) wants us to survive at all costs and so our ego tends to push us to put ourselves first at the expense of others.

Even the best of us have hurt others in our struggle to survive so we arrive in Summerland, faults and all.

This is why we have the life review. It gives us a chance to take a second look at our incarnation, see the kind, helpful things we did and also the harm we caused to others.

When we see the good that we did for others, this should gladden our hearts and our frequency rises somewhat.
When we see the harm we caused others, if we feel sorry for what we did those sins are wiped out.

We all make mistakes but if we feel sorrow for those mistakes, the errors are eradicated from us and our overall frequency rises.
If, however, we are glad for the harm we caused and are sorry that, in the higher 4th dimension, we can no longer cause more harm, our base frequency lowers.

So, to recapitulate. Before incarnation we form a life plan.
This, inevitably, whatever path we choose, will place us in situations where we must decide to harm others or to help them. So, in a way, the life plan will have little impact on the degree of good or bad we do.
Those choices come from the amount of ego we let develop.

Then, once incarnation finished we face our life review.
This gives us a second chance to modify our frequency.

We stress that at no point during any of these events does anyone judge us or try to influence us. We do it all ourselves according to whether we wish to follow the path of love or the path of hate.

Those who think that God judges us are mistaken.

Once the life review completed, our frequency is finally created by us.

You may remember us mentioning that in the heaven/hell area there were a vast number of levels, each one corresponding to a frequency and the lowest frequency ones being very bleak and the highest ones being very beautiful.
We also said that Summerland could be considered to be in the middle, the default zone.

Those of you who have lived in incarnation for any length of time will have surely noticed that people fall, by and large, into three categories.
There are a few very holy people, a few very horrible people, and then there is the vast majority of just decent people who do their best to live in peace together.
But, if you got to know really well a large number of people, you would notice that not only do they fall into these three categories that that no two people are exactly the same. They would all vibrate to slightly different frequencies.
Thus, to find a home for them in heaven/Summerland/hell, there needs to be a huge number of separate frequencies, one for each type of person.

Once the life review finished and once the final frequency decided upon - it happens naturally - then, by the law of mutual attraction, the person is drawn to a frequency (a landscape) that is closest to his own frequency.

Therefore, we can assume that hell contains a certain number of landscapes, heaven others but by far the largest area is Summerland as most people are ordinary although no two people are identical. Thus, there are a huge number of landscapes, some nicer than others, but each of a slightly different frequency. Just as many normal people incarnate are very similar so many of these frequencies are similar.

Therefore, large numbers of people drawn to Summerland are able to mix and to share life together.

But, as we go down to hell or up to heaven, not only are these areas kept apart from Summerland but each landscape tends to be apart from each other.
This also is due to natural law.

Therefore, we have these very low areas, each one of which is kept apart from any other. Then Summerland which tends to blend somewhat and then true heaven, a series of landscapes that tend to be kept apart.

We will, at this point, mention something very important.
Although each person develops a certain frequency that person is not stuck with that frequency for all eternity.
All have the freedom to raise or lower their frequency in which case they will move to higher or lower landscapes.
Generally speaking, people tend to try to raise their frequencies although it has been known for some people to be so steeped in negativity that they actively try to lower their frequency in which case they move to ever more sombre landscapes.
It might seem foolish to wish to become more evil instead of becoming more holy and it is of course foolish, but to use a well-known expression "It takes all sorts to make a world" and so there are people who seem to get enjoyment from being evil.
Thus, the lower they go the happier they are.
But most people try to become better people.

Now, there are a large number of people in the spirit world, the higher 4th dimension, that devote their lives to helping others rather as we try to help you and these people come down from their elevated plains and give lectures to try to explain a number of things about life to those lower on the ladder of life than them.

They would appear, to those lower than them, to shine with purity.
Life is light but the degree that someone shines to is commensurate to the degree of spirituality that the person has obtained.

Those that have had a near death experience often talk about being met by a person shining with pure light. To someone from Earth, to see a truly spiritual person would be to see that person as glowing with light.

We wish to repeat that when a person's incarnation finishes, with very few exceptions, that person will find himself in Summerland, the default zone of the heaven/hell complex. He will be met by someone who is there to greet the recently deceased person and will reassure the individual concerned that his incarnation has now finished and he is in the spiritual realms.

It might be worth mentioning that the spirit world takes no account of who the person was whilst incarnate.

A king or a pauper are exactly the same in spirit. Indeed, there has been many a situation in which a king or a very rich or highly respected person has died, has arrived in Summerland expecting to be waited on hand and foot, expecting to be given a palace to live in and has actually found himself, eventually, in one of the levels of hell, the result of having lead an egotistical, selfish and sometimes cruel life.

The same might apply to religious leaders of all types. If such a person lead a life of debauchery - and many of them did and still do - he will be drawn to a level of hell that corresponds to his level of unholiness.

A question often asked concerns the destiny of pet animals. Can they go off to our heaven?
The answer, quite simply, is yes!

Our system is based on love and love is a coming together emotion.
Anyone who has cared for a dog, for example, will know the high degree of love they can have for their owners and that they only ask to be loved in return.
Of course, there are a large number of pets of all sorts that display love in varying degrees.
But we wish to assure all pet owners that if they have a pet that they truly loved and that loved them, that pet will be there in heaven ready to continue the journey together.

Now, we mentioned love.
This implies that only people that have an affinity for each other will see each other.
The law of mutual attraction and its opposite, the law of mutual rejection, is always at work and so if you knew anyone that you did not like or get on with, you will not see that person in heaven.
It is a case of different vibrations keeping people apart.

We are considering the upper 4th dimension and have said that hell is part of the upper 4th and also part of what we might describe as heaven/Summerland/hell.
We will mention that, as its name implies, Summerland is so beautiful compared to anywhere on Earth that it relates more to the heavenly spheres than to the hellish ones.

There is much more to the upper 4th dimension then just the heaven/hell areas.
There are a large number of areas devoted to education.

No one is forced to educate themselves but for those that want to, every subject imaginable is available for study and to any level or degree the person concerned wishes to proceed to.

However, we must say that people who are in hell are barred from education. This is quite simply because education is a positive thing and falls under the vibrations of love. People in hell, by the very nature of their vibrations, are lower than that required by love vibrations. Thus, they bar themselves from education

If the day comes that people in hell are able, one by one, to repent their sins, they may rise to the higher spheres or landscapes and then they may join in educational groups.
We mentioned that every subject was available for study but there is a limit.
Subjects like pornography, terrorism and other negative concepts are not available generally. There are wise beings that keep an eye on such subjects so as to be aware of developments on Earth but students are not permitted to study them.

We mentioned that, by the law of mutual attraction, we would only see those to whom we feel attracted.
There are many groups of people, just to consider Summerland, that have widely differing personalities, egos and interests.
This automatically creates particular frequencies which means that individuals and groups vibrate at different frequencies. The result of this is that groups can be invisible to each other.
Thus, if we consider religious groups, different racial groups and on and on, if any one individual or group does not feel comfortable mixing with another individual or group, his vibration will be different and thus he would be invisible to another group.

For example, if a person is a Christian and another a Muslim and they do not feel comfortable mixing together their vibrations keep them apart. The same applies to race and so on

Then there is the situation in which people decide to come from higher spheres to teach or to go into the lower spheres (from true heaven to Summerland or to hell) in order to encourage those there to try to become better people. Normally, these people would be invisible to those lower than them due to the differences in vibrations so these people have to go through extensive training to learn to lower their frequency. This involves not pretending to be less holy but actually altering their personality DNA to become less holy.
This is not easy to do and involves actually becoming a person that they have struggled not to be for long years.

Having managed to lower their frequency somewhat enables them to become visible to lower groups and also to enter the dimension in which the lower people live.

To come from a high landscape down into Summerland does not take too much of a reduction but to be able to enter the depths of hell requires that the noble spirit actually rejects his nobility and takes on the feelings of evil people. The person has actually to become an evil person for a while in order to interact with those in any particular level of hell.

The lower the helper wishes to go the more he has to alter his frequency.
One could almost compare it to the story of Jekyll and Hyde.

Of course, once his mission is over the person is able to return to his former noble self but it is very unpleasant for them to go into these low areas to try to assist the poor souls stuck there, especially as any help is often rejected by those in hell.

Another area of the upper 4th dimension is devoted to animals once their incarnation is finished.
As we are all one, animals too go to the upper 4th.
They do not, generally, go to our Summerland - with the exception of beloved pets - but most animals go to an area set aside for them.

Once again, due to different frequencies, many groups are invisible to each other. Lions and other predatory animals would not be visible to herbivore animals. Fish would not be visible to land animals.
These animals stay in the upper 4th for a while after which their life essence slowly dissipates and the atoms recycled.

Plants have an area also and their life essence gets recycled like that of animals.

In principle there are areas for stones, water etc., but, in truth, these things last so long on Earth that we do not need to consider them.

We will say that in the upper 4th dimension there are areas for what you call aliens.
These beings are not exclusively in the upper 4th any more than life generally is.
Most life, whatever dimension it finds itself in, 7th or 4th maintains links to the 5th and 6th dimension as we have explained before.

We have not described all the life that is in the upper 4th dimension because there are a few life forms that we have never mentioned but we will stop in our investigation of that plain and briefly turn to the lower 4th.

CHAPTER 14

THE LOWER 4TH DIMENSION

We mentioned in the last chapter that this chapter would investigate the lower 4th dimension which, as a lot of students of esoteric wisdom know, is the area that contains the negative forces.

We have said that dimensions 1 and 2 also contain negative beings but they really do not concern us as the individuals in those dimensions have nothing to do with us. So, when we talk about negativity we may restrict ourselves exclusively to considering the lower 4th.

The lower 4th is a connected dimension to the upper 4th, the only difference as far as the dimension is concerned is frequency.

But, although both the lower and upper parts are separate it is only frequency that separates them. They are both part of one dimension - the 4th dimension.

However, what goes on in those two sub dimensions differs greatly.

We have explained that the upper 4th contains heaven and hell and, although hell can be very unpleasant, it is part of the upper 4th.

We have explained about the lower 4th in other books, talks and essays but, for those who do not regularly follow our talks and books, we will explain it all again perhaps, as we did in the last chapter, adding a few new items.

So, at the risk of repeating what we told you in a previous chapter, we will say that all the beings that end up in the lower 4th start off as points of life in the 8th dimension.

By hazard, some are selected to become the denizens of the lower 4th but first they are put into the 7th dimension as is all life.

There, gradually, they are given the DNA that will enable them to assume the role of creatures of destruction.

Once again, we will be repeating ourselves but for the sake of those who do not know, we will explain that we need both positive and negative beings in order to keep life in balance.

We will say something here that will be new to people incarnate because it is something that we have not discussed before.

To be honest, it is a subject that we have studiously avoided mentioning because it is something that sounds impossible.

In fact, if we consider what we need to say from a negative point of view first, it will be easier to understand what we need to say concerning the positive aspect.

You have all seen 'dead' things, we suppose. By dead, we mean plants that have died and are starting to rot, animals run over at the side of the road and some of you may even have seen dead people.

We have already explained that all that happens when something dies is that the life force separates from the physical body and goes off to the 4th dimension - the upper 4th. What actually happens is what is called a silver cord breaks (dissolves, actually) and so the link between the spirit force and the physical body is no longer maintained and the body stops living and the spiritual part goes off to Heaven.
Now, the bit that interest us from the point of view of this discussion is that the body, whether it be vegetable or flesh, starts to break down, to rot.

This seems so normal to us that we never question it.

Whether it is plants that have come to the end of their seasonal life, animals that have died for some reason or food forgotten at the back of a refrigerator, sooner or later food starts to rot.

The question is why should this be? What is the mechanism that changes a dead plant or a dead flesh and blood object from just being dead to turning into a stinking, slimy mess and finally decomposing entirely until, at the most, only a skeleton remains?

There are angelic beings in charge of this process and what they do is bombard the dead object with certain rays - vibrations - that have the effect of changing the frequency of the dead object from the natural frequency that all things on planet Earth vibrate to - the quiescent frequency of planet Earth - to a lower one.
Thus, the structure of the body of the plant or animal alters and, as it is no longer in harmony with planet Earth's vibration, it cannot maintain its integrity and, in effect, is rejected by the planet.
This seems strange and is not something that has ever been revealed before, as far as we are aware.

So, there are negative angels in the lower fourth dimension that constantly monitor living things and the moment they die, spring into action and bombarded things with this frequency, which causes dead things, effectively, to disappear thus preventing the land or the seas of planet Earth from being piled high with dead plants and/or animals, including dead humans.

Now, that is all very well and we are used to seeing dead things disappearing but, as all is one, there must be a process that makes living things grow.
Once again, we are used to seeing living things grow so we don't really question the process.

We know that if we take seeds, plant them, water them and give a certain amount of fertiliser, with a bit of luck the plants will grow.
Equally, we see babies of all kinds, animals or humans, and provided they are cared for, given food and liquids, they will grow to adulthood and then, finally, die.
Once again, we are so used to this process that we don't question it but, in fact, rather like the angels of destruction that we just described there are angels of construction that constantly bombard newborn creatures of all kinds with a ray (a vibration) that is just

slightly in excess of planet Earth's quiescent frequency that has the effect of drawing towards any living thing the atoms of that creature or plant and causing it to grow.

If this were not the case the atoms would not be attracted to whatever it is that needs to grow.
This is new information and, we must admit, sounds improbable but, like everything else that we tell you, is true.

These angelic forces are contained within the 4th dimension. The angels for construction are within the upper 4th and the angels for destruction are within the lower 4th.

In the case of the angels of construction, young creatures are bombarded with this frequency of a greater power than when it approaches adulthood. As the entity approaches adulthood the strength of the rate is reduced so, in infancy, when the ray is strong, the infant grows quickly but from adulthood onwards the ray is reduced so that the entity does not grow much at all.
It can happen, if an object reaches great age, that it starts to get bombarded by both rays at once, albeit both of a very limited power. This has the effect of the object staying alive but part of the physical body deteriorating.
We see this in some trees, some animals and some humans who reach great age but their physical bodies start to decay causing all sorts of illnesses.
But let us return to the lower 4th dimension.

We mentioned the angels of destruction because the lower 4th dimension is largely concerned with destruction just as the upper 4th is concerned with love which relates to construction.
This is not to say that the lower 4th is connected to hate although humans that are consumed with hate can use the beings contained within the lower 4th dimension to put into operation their evil plans.

Now, the aim of this book is, by and large, to discuss personality although we take the opportunity to expand somewhat and introduce other topics some more or less directly related to personality.

The problem is that, as all is one, all is connected and so, as we are discussing one topic this often leads us onto others.
If we think that these extra topics are somewhat relevant and that you might find them interesting we mention them at the risk of making this book rather large and possibly confusing.

However, if you have followed out other teachings you should be able to follow along. We will add one further comment here if we may.

Much of what we tell you is complicated and some of it is new and maybe above your level of comprehension. If this is the case, please do not let it worry you.

These books are given now but we hope will remain in circulation for many long years into the future and so, as people evolve, their level of comprehension will grow and so that which seems confusing now will become obvious in the future.

Once again, we got sidetracked!
Let us return to the lower 4th, the creatures that reside there and their personalities.

Unlike the upper 4th, the lower 4th is not concerned with incarnation above and beyond destroying dead objects, as we mentioned above.
Also, there is no concept of heaven and hell. It tends to be one area.

However, it contains a sufficient number of life-forms to fulfill the requirements of keeping dead and dying objects under control, which is why it exists.
The positive regions that we have mentioned at great length in this and other works can be intricate indeed but the actions emitting from the lower 4th are much more simple. Construction is always more complicated than destruction. For instance, it may take months to construct a house, but, with explosives, can take a second to destroy it.

So, there are a number of negative creatures in the lower 4th, each one or each group programmed to destroy a particular aspect of creation in order to keep all in balance.
These creatures, that we tend to call devils, have been carefully trained to fulfil a particular function.
Now, religion tends to connect these devils with the negative aspects of some humans but that is because some evil people have learnt to harvest the negative energies of these beings to cause harm to positive people.

In fact, the devils are trained to control destruction.
Whether it is just disposing of dead and dying life forms on Earth or whether their power is harnessed to cause mayhem on Earth is not the fault of these devils.
They do their job which is always destruction and do not have the ability to pick and choose for whom they work.
They are not given sufficient personalities to pick and choose.
If they receive a message that they should destroy something, whether it be a dead plant or the life and health of someone, they spring into action and perform that duty. The people to blame are the black magicians who harness their energy.

But let us delve into the lower fourth and see what it looks like and what is going on.

Those of you who have developed the ability to enter Summerland in the upper 4th or have had a NDE would have immediately noticed a few things.
They will be aware that they have entered an area of bright light, warmth and beauty.
So, it does not require much intelligence to work out that the lower 4th is the complete opposite.

Those who enter the lower 4th will be aware of Stygian darkness. It is pitch black there.

Temperature does not seem to play a great role but we can say that it is not the least bit warm.

The next thing we notice is a feeling of abject terror. In the upper 4th we are surrounded by love but in the lower 4th we are surrounded by terror.
It is a feeling that has to be experienced in order to appreciate.
So great is this feeling of terror that many visitors from the higher 4th dimension cannot stay there. It is literally indescribable.

Now, although it is pitch dark, such is the nature of the astral world that visitors can, nevertheless, see.
So what would they observe?

First, there is no life as we know it in the sense of plants, rivers, lakes etc.
It is all just a barren wasteland.

Now, we must mention the beings that live there - the devils.

Like all life, due to their personalities, they tend to vibrate to various frequencies.
So a visitor to the lower 4th might not be able to see all that lives there due to an incompatibility with the visitor's frequency.

However, we will try to describe them.
We have to say that no devil resembles the pictures you may have seen of devils as presented by religions.
Nor is there a king devil variously known as Satan, old Nick etc.
But devil's there are and of various degrees of power.
But they do not have any form of physicality. They are orbs of what we might call light.

Now, once again we must introduce you to a concept that you will not know about although man should have had the intelligence to work this out.

Light is vibration (frequency). The higher the frequency the brighter the light gets.
And it is a positive frequency.

However, there is more to life than that.

There is a negative counterpart that we might call a negative frequency.
So light can exist but is observed as a negative light by which we mean that, as positive light manifests itself in ever-increasing frequency, so negative light manifests itself in degrees of ever-increasing negative frequencies.

This may be difficult to comprehend but if we take pitch-black as a starting point, positive light starts with the slightest glimmer and increases to the light of the sun or a star.
Equally, people, angels etc., glow with similar degrees of brilliance.

Now, from pitch black there is another version of light that starts off with pitch black and gets ever darker.
Because of the way our eyes work, we cannot see this negative light but it exists.
Similarly, negative creatures correspond to degrees of this negative light.

The more negative a being is the more it radiates negative light.
This cannot readily be seen with the naked eye but for those trained in psychic vision it can be observed as ever darker patches or orbs of darkness.
So, when we are in the lower 4th dimension, depending on our skill to operate in the esoteric realms, it might be possible to observe orbs floating about of various degrees of negative light.
The more powerful a devil is the more negative light he would emit.

When these orbs, these devils, are in their domain, the lower 4th, they can cause no harm to humans and even if we are foolish enough to go into their realm, generally they will not harm us. But it must be said that going into the lower 4th is a bit like going into a lion's den.

You may be aware that in the upper 4th dimension there are all sorts of positive beings. If we ignore humans that are there, there remain a large number of creatures that range from quite low powered beings, through the angels up to extremely powerful archangels.
They are all there to serve God in keeping his kingdom in growth.

Equally and oppositely, in the lower 4th there are a large number of negative entities ranging from low powered up to and including negative angels and negative archangels. Their function also is to keep God's Kingdom in order but not from growth but from the point of view of clearing up the mess caused by things dying.
So they are equally as important as the positive angels and life would be chaotic if they did not exist constantly clearing up the debris left by dying entities.

We have no doubt that many readers are curious to know the names that are attributed to these negative individuals or groups. This is not easy because, although there are a large number of them ranging from almost harmless to extremely powerful, they do not really have names anymore than the positive forces do.
But we will try to explain a little.

You may have heard of djinns.
These tend to be quite low powered compared to true demons, the negative equivalent of Archangels.
But they exist and have varying degrees of negative power, some more than others.

The function is to instigate the destructive process of plants and other easily disposed of objects. The harder a flora would be to dispose of - a tree for instance - the more powerful a group of djinn would be dispatched to deal with it.
A blade of grass would only require the attention of a low powered djinn.

But these djinn have developed the ability to transform into objects that we can see. Although they have a destructive function, like all things they have free will and can move into physicality, or a replica of it.

They also have curiosity and like to ape sentient animals and even humans.

So, if and when they are seen, they might just be seen as grey orbs or they might be observed in the form of cats, dogs, rabbits and other animals or even as a sort of human although they are not very good at aping human morphology.

The striking feature about djinn is, if alarmed, they will return to the astral realms by forming a sort of black, smokeless smoke, if that makes sense, from their rear or lowest end and, in a flash, transforming into invisibility by drawing that smoke into themselves from the lowest exterior towards the head and in a second they are gone.

It is difficult to describe but is impressive to watch.

This smokeless smoke is, of course, them returning to the darkness of their natural colour - negative light.

They can be used by black magicians, and often are although they have no loyalty to the magician and will be equally content to harm the magician as his intended victim.

The image of a djinn is often used in the children's tale of 'The Genie in the Lamp' and the djinn can be seen with a vaguely human head and torso but the rest of his body as smoke.

We will try to explain somewhat about a true demon - the equivalent of an archangel.

Once again, they were points of life that started out in the 8th dimension, were given the logos by God and moved to the 7th.

By now, it knew that it was going to be part of the negative forces.

In the 7th dimension it was given the necessary DNA to help form it into a demon, went through the relative orb galaxy and became a fully-fledged negative archangel (a demon) and finished up in the lower 4th dimension from which it fulfils is function of decomposing 'dead' things.

Now, really powerful demons do not concern themselves with clearing up dead grass and things like that. They would be kept in reserve for dealing with very serious events like cataclysms.

All of these various demonic forces can be harvested by man but the more powerful a demon is the more difficult and dangerous it is to deal with them.

Any black magician should be aware that the function of a demon is to destroy and any demonic force would be just as happy destroying him as it would any victim.

We will not describe the steps needed to be taken by a black magician for controlling djinns or demons but we will say that, sooner or later, the power of the magician will fade and he will almost certainly fall victim to the negative influence of the negative entity he is trying to control.

There is an aspect of life that should be obvious but that few neophyte magicians ever seem to consider.

If a person wishes to study the esoteric arts, whether he desires to perfect what we might call white magic (although it is not magic but physics) or whether he desires to perfect black magic, he needs to follow a similar path, although in the desire to achieve opposite results.

Anyone desirous of following the path of light will, as we have often explained, need to do three things.
1. Pray to almighty God, thanking him for the blessings he sends.
2. Meditate on a regular basis which opens the path to connection to the Higher Self.
3. Aid and assist all life when appropriate.

These three simple acts will, over time, open the doors to all the positive acts and attributes that man calls the gifts of the spirit.

A black magician follows exactly the same path although instead of his aim being to raise his vibrational frequency, thus enabling him to approach the white light - starlight of God - his aim would be to develop power to harm people.

As his skills increase, so his vibrational frequency drops and he lowers his frequency towards blackness - the opposite of the starlight of God.

Now, the law of mutual attraction is always at work drawing like to like.
You may know that you are never alone.
Even if you live in a cave you always have spiritual entities that watch over you rather as a child is watched over by his parents.
Even children abandoned by their Earth parents will never be abandoned by their spiritual 'parents'.
The fact is that basically we are all one and the fact that we have a certain frequency causes, by the law of mutual attraction, certain spiritual humans to be drawn towards us and us to them. We must also remember that we are part of a soul group and that soul group will always stay linked to us whether we be in incarnation or not.
Thus we are never alone.

As our frequency increases through following the path of holiness so the beings that we attract to us will also be of ever higher frequency until, if we are actively engaged in spiritual work assisting our fellow man, the beings associated with us could be called angels.

We must mention that, to do God's work, it is not necessary to become known publicly. It suffices to live quietly and correctly, meditate and, above all, help all life when it is appropriate. Then, gradually, our frequency rises and such people can, by the law of mutual attraction, be surrounded by angels.

Thus, we wish to assure all good people that you may never be known publicly, may never have any sort of public recognition but if you just spend your life following the 3 precepts given above; thanking God, meditating for a few minutes each day and being of

service to all life; humans, animals and even Flora (plants), your frequency will rise and you will attract ever higher spirit guides as they are known.
Thus you will be helped through your incarnation by evermore holy guides and your place in heaven is assured.

We perhaps should, before we return to discussing the lower 4th and black magicians, add a warning that we have mentioned before.
There are people who start out following the correct path to God that we mentioned above but find that they achieve a certain fame and who fall into the trap of allowing their ego to influence them.
As one advances along the path it usually happens that the gifts of the spirit, as they are known, start to appear.
These gifts are much admired by those whom we might consider ordinary people.
Thus, the person who finds that he or she has a certain control of these gifts is tempted to exploit them. He might write books, give lectures and/or give private readings for which he charges money.
Now, the gifts of the spirit are gifts given freely by God to those willing to follow the path of righteousness. But they are gifts and they are freely given by God so that the recipient of these gifts may impart spiritual wisdom to lesser people. The thing is that they are freely given and should be freely shared.

If a person uses those gifts with the desire to seek fame or fortune, God reserves the right to remove those gifts … and he will!
One should never be tempted to use the gifts to seek fortune or financial remuneration.

But let us return to black magicians.

We described how a person following the path to God must act.
People following the opposite path do exactly the same except in the opposite sense.
Instead of praying to 'our' God they pray to Satan, the devil.
What they don't perhaps know is that Satan is just a thought form.
God, although invisible, is real. It is the only thing that is real but Satan is just an invention of religions.
So, those who pray to Satan are just praying to an empty thought, which is foolish.
They meditate but with the intention of developing the gifts of the devil. As the devil does not exist, it is difficult to know what gifts they hope to develop!
Lastly, instead of helping all life they try to harm life. Thus they perform human and animal sacrifices and other things of a harmful nature.
The result of all this is to lower their frequency and, by the law of mutual attraction, they draw towards them beings from the lower 4th - Djinn and demons, depending on how far they lower their frequency.

Naturally, when their incarnation is finished they are drawn to the depths of Hell.

But, when incarnate, as their frequency lowers and as they are surrounded by harmful creatures, so their health and their lives suffer.

One outstanding example is the most famous black magician of modern times. We will not mention his name. He came from a very rich and famous family but ended his life prematurely a pauper and in poor health. Further, this unfortunate man is now in hell repaying the debt to society he incurred in his incarnation.
This is the inevitable reward for devoting one's life to following the wrong path.
No one made him do this. It was his own free choice. But it shows that to follow any path that is not of a holy path will end in destruction.

Thus we wish to make it quite clear to all of you who read this book that you have free will.
No one will interfere in your life choices.
Life is meant to be experienced and you may experience it as you will.
But, equally, there is a price for everything.
To try to advance on Earth at the expense of others is, of course, permitted as it is your choice but will ultimately result in a heavy price to pay.

This price is not a judgement. No one judges you ever in the spirit realms. There is no need.
You automatically rise or fall in vibration as you live your life and thus, when you get to the spirit realms - and indeed, to a certain extent in physicality - you will draw towards you the landscape and the type of life commensurate to that vibration.
Thus, in a sense you judge yourself or at least you create the conditions which permit you to be drawn to a certain landscape.

Having explained that, one would expect most, if not all, people to follow the path of righteousness, but how many actually do?
Enormous numbers of people are engaged in negative activities; crimes of all sorts.
Others are engaged in selling inferior goods to gullible people.
Yet others are engaged in military, police and prison activities which, whilst perhaps necessary, are hardly the best path to peace and love.

We could go on but we have said enough.
All we can do is to advise you to follow the path to God and you will attract God's angels to you who will guide and protect you.
Only if you allow your ego and personality to push you down the road of evil will you meet creatures from the lower 4th who will guide you further down the path of evil.
Don't forget, the function of devils is to destroy. They will be just as happy destroying you as they would any victim you might wish to harm.

Even in the best scenarios, according to the way you lead and lead your life, if you follow evilness you will lower your vibrations, draw bad things towards you now and will finish up in the low regions of Heaven.
All this can be avoided by being a nice person and putting others ahead of you.
Jesus said,' Love thy neighbour as thyself.'
What he meant was,' Do unto others as you would have them do unto you.'
Equally, 'Never do to others that which you would not like done to you.'

If you treat all life with love, by the law of mutual attraction, you will draw love towards you.
Gradually, step-by-step, as you follow the path in peace, gentleness and love, your personality will improve and you will become a better person.
Inevitably, your frequency will rise and you will attract evermore holy spirit guides to you who will assist you to become a yet more holy person.

Through the law of mutual attraction and its counterpart the law of mutual rejection, good people draw good things into their lives but, by the same token, cause bad things to happen with less frequency.

As we live in this so-called physical world, inevitably, problems will arise from time to time but a holy person can draw positive forces to his aid.

Now, in this book, we have attempted to explain some of how personalities develop and the effects that they have on our lives.
We have not explained all.
Life is complex, and as all is connected, to fully explain personalities we would need to unravel all of life and that would fill the most enormous book ever written.
Life is endless and personality is an important part of life. The more advanced a being is, the more his personality is important. Thus, humans, as they advance, develop stronger and stronger personalities.
If one were lucky enough to meet a human archangel, his personality would be overwhelming.
This, obviously, is a positive personality and it can happen that the personality of the archangel is so strong that it can overpower a person who is seeking guidance from him and, effectively, push away the seekers auras and have them replaced by the auras of the archangel.
So the archangel and the seeker of guidance become one for a short time.
This seems very strange but it can happen. The seeker might be carnate or incarnate but if he is overpowered by a good human archangel, the archangel can, effectively, replace the seeker's auras and thus his personality, and so the archangel and the ordinary person become one.

If and when this happens in a positive sense, the result is positive and the seeker can act almost like an archangel until he withdraws, in which case the seeker returns to himself.
But, should the same thing occur and a powerful demon take over the personality of a black magician, the magician can act for and with the same power as the demon.
Thus, the demon and magician might be able to accomplish remarkable things for the duration of the overshadowing, but once the demon withdraws, the magician feels exhausted, having used all his reserves of energy to produce the works he wanted.

We hope that you can see that the difference between two people, one of whom is following the part of holiness and the second the path of evil, is largely the same path.

The only real difference is direction. One aims to help life and the other aims to harm life.
These different paths are, of course, the result of personality.
Two people having virtually the same training but, as a result of different personalities becoming totally different people.

We could say much the same concerning positive or negative angels or archangels.
They too follow very similar paths but the direction of their education being opposed.
One is taught holiness and the other evil.

We must stress a difference between the two groups of angelic beings, the first inhabiting the upper 4th and the second the lower 4th, and it is this.

In the upper 4th the angelic beings are only too willing to share their knowledge with those lesser than them including you and us, but in the lower 4th this does not happen.
By spiritual law, living a holy life is to recognise that all is one and so it is important to share all wisdom with all good people.
But in the lower 4th dimension, such is the nature of evilness that sharing information is not part of personality.
Higher evil beings sharing information with lower beings does not normally happen and thus, should a black magician wish to learn from a devil, he must strike a bargain, give something, perform some evil act in order to be given information.

Had he taken the path of righteousness, he could have freely got similar or the same information from holy angels without having to strike a bargain but such is the nature of black magicians that they think that everything has to be paid for. Which is why they hold their disgusting rituals called black masses.

Another aspect of the lower 4th that would be remiss not to mention is the UFO aspect.
We have mentioned this before.

Now, many long years ago, life was in the depths of the negative swing of this pendulum of life and so, life on Earth was in the grips of negativity.
We must say that this was before the human group who are on Earth at the moment came to be.
The group that were on Earth at that time were very advanced technical logically but tended to be drawn towards evil.
Thus, a group of negative angels wondered if they could possibly enter 3D Earth environment and so, with the help of some Earth scientists, created the UFOs that are sometimes seen flying around the skies.
They all the same machines, or duplicates of them, that were invented all that long time ago.

The demons also invented little robots and are still creating them today.

It must be realised that the UFOs and the robots have two aspects to them.

They can be astral or they can lower their frequency and appear in our world.

But it must be remembered that they are negative. Not so much the UFOs that are just machines but the little robots are under the psychic control of demons so, if you are contacted by these creatures, bear in mind that behind them and controlling them are demons.

We feel that we have explained enough about the lower 4th dimension.
So we will stop here and close this chapter.

CHAPTER 15

2 TYPES OF PERSONALITIES

We wish to investigate another aspect of personality that is seldom considered.
It has to do with the way that individual personalities link in a cosmic sense. By which we mean that all people incarnate or discarnate have individual personalities which they have developed over time but, at the same time, these personalities link together to form global personalities.
So, let us expand on this until we can fully understand.

Although each and every person has a distinct personality, nevertheless, people can be grouped into personality types.
For instance, we might have nice people. We might have nasty people. We might have those drawn towards science, medicine, education and so on.
So, although, if we got to know any group, each individual would be unique in that he would have a particular personality, nevertheless, those people would share a common aspect for any particular aspect of life and those common aspects we could consider to be an aspect of personality.

This may not seem obvious at first glance but, for instance, there are people who devote their entire lives to politics.
Now, politics is a very fraught career path to follow.
First it requires that one has an exaggerated opinion of self. It also requires great cunning.
Also, a person who desires to enter politics needs to have enormous degrees of energy and stamina so as to be able to battle on during election campaigns, touring from city to city giving speeches, taking very little rest and, somehow, finding the energy to soldier on, often against all odds.
It is worth bearing in mind that, if there is an election somewhere, no matter how many people are vying to get elected, only one person can be elected.
Then, a few years later it all starts again.

Even if someone is lucky enough to get elected, when he comes to the end of his elected time it will be obvious to both him and to his constituents that he has achieved nothing. But he must stand up in front of his constituents and admit that he might have failed last time but try to convince the voters that this time he really does have the answers and so, if the public vote for him again, he will solve all their problems.

It takes a very special person to be able to face a public, having failed over and over again and still try to convince people that he knows what he is doing.
But such is the ego of politicians that they carry on without hesitation, pushing and pushing to try to get people to vote for them.

Equally, and this is the interesting part, there are large numbers of people - potential voters - who are willing to put their trust in someone who has failed over and over again.

But, through sweet talking, the electors are willing to put their common sense on hold and vote for someone who has no idea what he is doing.
So, it is often the case that large numbers of voters accept into their personalities the personality of the particular politician.
This is interesting because, if we look back over the history of any particular group of politicians or a political party, at no stage is the public actually helped. The only people who have been helped are the individual politicians who are paid large salaries, plus exorbitant expense accounts to pay for apartments, hotels, restaurants and travel expenses.
The actual voters get nothing in return for voting for a politician.
And yet the voters seem perfectly happy to vote for a person or a party and will laudit the virtues of a person or a party, incorporating the individual or collective personality of a politician or a party into their personality.

The same applies to religions of course. Equally, we find people with strong nationalistic pride who, without hesitation, will join an army to fight a supposed enemy, the dangers of whom are extolled by small groups of people who have a vested interest in encouraging people to think like them.

If we think about this it seems strange that one person - or a small group of people - with a strong personality can overpower huge numbers of the public with lesser personalities and the public incorporate that person's personality into their own personality.
So it might be interesting to try to analyse what is going on.

You may remember us talking about the fact that personality is actually DNA and that DNA is stored in the akashic record and is loaned to individuals. We have also explained that there were two aspects to personalities.
1. The different types of personality that we choose according to our different and varying interests.
2. The power that we develop of these personality trends.

But there is more to personality than just the fact that the types of personality trends are stored in the akashic record and are loaned to people.

The personalities are taken - on loan, so to speak - from the akashic record and are copied into the various auras.
Before we go on explaining this we remind you that the auras are multitasking and perform all sorts of duties and distributing our personality aspects throughout the various auras is one of them.

Therefore, many of our auras - not all of them - are influenced by the DNA that concerns personalities and are connected to our auras.
But the thing about auras is that, whilst each and every one of us is influenced by our auras, the auras also act in a more global sense in that we are all connected via our auras. The auras act both in an individual sense and in a collective sense.
Our DNA is connected to our auras and thus our personalities are connected to our auras.

You may remember us saying that if you were contacted by an archangel, it may happen that the power of his personality would be so strong that it would push your auras aside and his auras would overtake you - overshadow you.

Powerful people incarnate; politicians, religious leaders, trade unionists and other 'leaders' can do the same to a certain extent.
They may not have the power of an archangel and they certainly would not have the wisdom but they have sufficient power to be able to influence the auras of undeveloped people and thus to push them to think like them and, if necessary, to vote for them.

So, to a certain extent one of these leaders can reach out, push weak people's auras aside and replace them with their own twisted views.
This is obviously not a good idea because, in effect, instead of the public being able to decide for themselves which path to follow on any subject the public are being forced to think like any leader to which they feel drawn.
Now, all people have their own basic personalities and thus will naturally feel sympathetic to certain parties, right wing, centre or left, or drawn to any religion but when, on top of their own policies, they are being brainwashed by powerful politicians who, effectively, reinforce any person's basic views, that person becomes convinced that his point of view is the correct and only valid point of view.

This is why there are so many ordinary people who are convinced that a certain political point of view is the correct one, any religion is obviously correct and so on.

The fact that these leaders might, in turn, be under the influence of archons or negative forces does not help.
There are, unfortunately, a number of leaders all over the world that are being fed negative information by a variety of negative entities in the astral realms so that these leaders are expressing, in part, their own views and, in part, the views of negative beings and who, in turn can influence, in part, their own views formed by their own personalities but mixed with the views of leaders who, in turn, are expressing in part, the views of evil spirits, the net result is that whole swathes of the world's population finish up spouting the views of evil forces.

This is why the world is in such a mess.
The general public are always seeking guidance but the only people to whom they can turn are these so-called leaders. If these leaders are spouting information given to them by evil spirits in order to harm the world, we are going in the wrong direction.

This has gone on for long enough.
During the long ages when the world was in the negative part of the biological clock effect known as ascension - or perhaps we should use an opposite term - decline - nothing could be done about it but now we are truly entering the positive aspect - ascension.
It is time that old time politicians or religious leaders saw that they are spouting nonsense and either retired or turned to meditation to fill their auras with positivity.

But it is not in the nature of politicians or religious leaders to admit to going in the wrong direction. Nor is it likely for them to retire.
Power, it is said, is the greatest aphrodisiac. This is true and it is easy to work out why but we will not investigate that aspect of life.
With power, generally, comes money.
Money and power generate respect.
Thus, anyone in power can live in a world where he is surrounded by people willing to do his slightest bidding.
Magnificent houses to live in.
The finest food.
The finest clothes.
Chauffeur driven limousines,
first class train tickets,
first class air tickets,
top hotels.
It goes on and on and politicians and other leaders quickly become accustomed to this way of life and will cling on tooth and nail rather than admit any failure.
One can understand this but, unfortunately for them, the pendulum swing into positivity is ineluctable and so, sooner or later, they will be voted out and their places taken by positive leaders.
This will take time as the pendulum swing is very slow but it will happen and nothing will stop it.

There will be two noticeable effects from this change.
The first will be that those leaders, when they lose their positions of power, will find themselves in exactly the same position as the working classes they exploited for all those years and will struggle to make ends meet.
The second will be that the masses that were influenced in a negative fashion by negative leaders will now be influenced in exactly the same manner by positive leaders.
So, their point of view will take a 180° change but less strong-willed people will still be influenced by strong-willed people - but in a positive sense.
This will be a good thing but it does show that weak-willed people can always be influenced by strong-willed people.

So, strong willed people will always be setting the tone, so to speak, and weak-willed people will follow.

We said that a powerful archangel can overshadow less strong-willed people, push their auras away and replace them with the auras of the strong-willed archangel.
This can happen in the Heavenly spheres and will certainly happen on Earth.
The question one must ask is if this is a good thing or not?

One would suppose that, as we are all one, we would all be equal but, from what we have told you above, it is not so.

Some people, both good and bad, have stronger wills, stronger personalities then others and a strong-willed person, through his auras, can influence the auras of large numbers of others. So, whole masses of people can be influenced by the will of a single person or, indeed, a group of strong-willed people working together in a common aim.

This, of course, puts a great burden on any strong-willed person or group to consider in which direction that person must proceed.

A good person or group must ensure that he only acts for good as his every move, every thought is influencing large numbers of people.

It can happen that a good, strong willed person strays from the path of righteousness, in which case, as those being influenced for good by the will, the personality of the first person, discover the change of direction, feel very disappointed, very let down by the leader and that causes the masses to lose hope.

Therefore, it is of the utmost importance that anyone who finds himself in a position of leader going in a positive direction, must never relaxes vigilance, never grow tired of acting as leader and, no matter how tired he becomes, always remembers his position as leader and always puts his followers first and himself last.

We must remember that there are an equal number of strong willed, strong personalitied people acting in a negative sense - although their number will decrease as we move into ascension - and they are affecting masses of weak-willed people to produce negativity.

Will, as we have mentioned in other books, is the desire to create and put an idea into action.
So, will is closely connected to Higher Self and is also connected to personality and its DNA and also connected to auras.
As everyone's auras are constantly broadcasting thoughts out of the world it is only the degree of development, of power, that controls the influence one person can have on others.

Nevertheless, it is important that all people, regardless of the power of their personality, behave at all times in a positive manner because his auras are influencing others and even, to a certain extent, influencing a strong-willed person.

So, in an ideal sense, it seems to us that the more people that are doing good, the more that makes the job of a good leader easy.

This is the system we have in heaven.
There are groups of angels and archangels influencing lesser beings but these lesser beings are encouraged constantly to think noble thoughts and, in that manner, heaven becomes the wonderful place it is.

As we rise in ascension and as angels and archangels draw close to you incarnate, it behoves all good people to do the best they can to be holy and, together, angels, archangels, we in the Heavenly spheres and you incarnate will make planet Earth a better place for all to live in.

We must also state that, in the lower 4th dimension, there are an equal number of demonic forces as there are positive forces in the upper 4th.
If it were not for a certain number of black magicians who attempt to employ these demonic forces to harm people incarnate, they would not be a problem to us.
However, those who have power and wish to cling onto it sometimes employ demonic forces and thus cause a certain amount of harm.

Then we have archons who only know negativity and a certain number of negative reptilians who try to cause harm.

But, as life marches on and as many negative humans die off to go to their home in hell, so they are being replaced with better people. So, inevitably, life will improve.

This chapter is short but we wished to draw your attention to those beings - positive and negative - who have powerful personalities and can influence large numbers of ordinary people.

It is all well and good being influenced by good and holy powerful people but we wished to bring to your attention the number of people of powerful will and personality who do not have your best interests at heart and use you to promote their own self interests.

We advise you not to follow these people and not to vote for politicians and not to follow church leaders if you suspect that they might be putting their interests above yours and are merely using you to get the votes or the finance that they need to keep themselves in power over you.

They need you but you do not need them.
By not voting for such people or for not financing them will force them out of positions of influence and their places may be taken by good people.

CHAPTER 16

NOTHING IS SOMETHING

Let us turn to another aspect of personality and this will examine how our personal and collective personalities join together to create the world we live in because, do not think that your personality just stops with you.
As we have said, all is one although, as we explained in the last chapter, we all have personalities in varying degrees of power.
Therefore, as we have also said, we are constantly, through our auras, broadcasting thoughts out to the world.
Further, these thoughts also go out to every corner of all of creation, the physical, the astral realms and on into the furthest outreaches of every part of creation.

We don't know if you can imagine this?

Every thought that you have is not only being stored for all eternity in the akashic record but wings its way out forever into every part of the immense multiverse that God and his archangels - the directors of life - have created.

You may imagine that in the various books, videos and essays that we have so far given you that we are getting close to describing all that exists.
You would be wrong.
We cannot say how much of creation we have so far described to you in terms of all that exists but if we said that, so far, we have described 1% of creation, that would be a fair estimate.
Having said that, it would also be fair to say that some aspects of life are so different from what we can expect you to understand that it would be pointless in undertaking the task of describing all of creation to you.
We will also admit that there are areas that we do not truly understand - life is endless - so even the wisest of us have to declare forfeit after a while.

But even in these deepest, hardest to understand parts of consciousness people's thoughts reach and these thoughts can have positive or negative effects on life.
So please accept that in this chapter we may well describe events and actions that may be difficult to accept.
Accept what you can and place what you can't understand at the back of your mind until the light does shine on it and its meaning becomes clear.

So let us begin to dissect how people's personalities affect life.

If you have read and understood all that we have told you in previous chapters of this quite long and complicated book, you may be ready to take this next step.
If you are not ready, until you do understand what we told you earlier, you may struggle with this chapter and, indeed, any following chapters.

But we have to make some bizarre and startling claims.
From what we told you in earlier chapters of this book you may have picked up that personality is of great importance and is linked to DNA (which invades the vast area not only of people, animals, plants and minerals but also links to virtually every aspect of life: Higher Self, will, imagination and all the countless aspects of life).
Personalities made well be stored in the Akash but, as was described concerning the personality orbs, stretches out into galaxies that are known as the signs of the zodiac.
And it goes on and on.

Our task in this chapter is to describe as best we can some of the outreaches of personality.

We will jump in at the deep end which is not something that we usually like to do.
We prefer to proceed slowly and getting to the main point being made after we have given good cause as to why the point we are making is acceptable.
But, in this case we are going to make a statement and try to justify it later.

The point we wish to make in this chapter is that, if it was not for personalities, the galaxies would be empty. There would be no creation, no life. The various dimensions would just be empty carrier waves bereft of any form of life.

In view of all that we have told you in the past about how life is created and organised it would seem unlikely that mere personalities would play such a capital role in creation but, after we have explained, we hope that you will be able to appreciate the logic of what we said.

If you go back over the chapters of this book you will be reminded of how the Holy Spirit was able to take the single God force and create, via DNA, countless life forces that resulted in everything - and we mean everything - that has been, is or ever will be.
This DNA, as we have said many times, is involved in the creation of personality.
So, we have a clear trace back from personalities to the God force itself.
We could stop this chapter here because we have said, in a nutshell, what the connection is but we hope you will forgive us if we spend a few lines expanding somewhat.

The question is where do we start?
Life, as we have often said, is like a wheel turning tracing a straight line in the mud.
So, life appears to be a straight line which is measured as time and space but, if we could step back far enough we would see it actually as a never-ending wheel, forever turning.
We could question which part is true, the straight line or the wheel but when we realise that it is the wheel that creates the line in the mud it is obvious which part of creation is true.
What, perhaps, is hard to comprehend is that the wheel part is immense and it turns so slowly that countless eons of time pass before the wheel returns to its point of origin.
But turn it does and has been doing so for so long that it is fair to say that no one knows for how long it has been turning.

If life is like a wheel turning, we might ask what force is motivating the wheel? After all, nothing works by magic and if we can find the force that makes the wheel turn we would expect to be able to understand the physics behind this force that causes the rotation.
We might even be able to comprehend the nature of this force in the sense of is it electric or some other power source?

It is said that God created everything and this might be true in our galaxy but, as we have found out through our investigations, our God is not the only one.
Behind the various Gods we developed the concept of a master creator coordinating the paths that the various Gods take.
Now, we don't like the idea of a master creator because it provokes the idea that is there just one master creator and if there are more, how many creator Gods are there?
Are there an infinite number of Gods stretching endlessly backwards in creation?

We will be honest and say to you that there is strong evidence of a creator God but beyond that we do not know.
And, to be honest, we are not even sure that the creator God created Gods. We call him a creator God because we assume that he created all that exists but we cannot confirm if he created Gods nor do we know who created the creator God.

Gods just seem to be and yet this is not an answer.
Nothing appears like magic although we have had to accept that our God, at least, seems always to have existed.
This, also, is not a satisfactory answer.
If something exists it has to have come from somewhere or been created by someone.
And yet we really struggle to find answers to these questions.

Is there any way of resolving this or these questions?

Apparently, before there was God - any God - there was nothing.
So we are back to the impossible question. How can something - God - be created from nothing?
It presupposes that there must have been something. But what could have been that something?
Was it another God somewhere?
We have mentioned a super God that works in many areas far remote from us. But then who created that God? The question cannot be answered like that because we just go on quoting God after God like a record stuck in a groove.
Common sense tells us that that cannot be right.
If so, how many creator Gods are there? Ten, one hundred, one thousand? Where does that end?
So we feel that we must look in another direction to find a creator God's origin.

Once we have a creator God, of course, the rest of creation may start to fit together like the Jigsaw we mentioned. It is finding the start of creation that is hard and yet there must have been a start because we are all here.

So, our task, if it is possible, is to try to discover who created this giant wheel of life and who gave it the initial push to get it turning because they may not be the same entity. Also, as a bonus, perhaps we can find what energy keeps the wheel turning.

We hope that you all realise that when we mention the wheel of life we are speaking metaphorically.
There is no wheel but there is a force that came from somewhere and created all that exists and our investigations have shown that life proceeds for a while at which point it all stops and starts again as if it were a wheel turning. The old end joins to a new beginning so to speak.

We said that there was no point in chasing after creator Gods because a problem can only be solved from a higher frequency than the problem itself and looking at and into Gods will not reveal where they came from.
And yet they came from somewhere and were created by something.

Let us try to cut to the chase, to use a modern colloquialism, and say that God did not create us.
We created God through our personalities. This sounds like craziness but bear with us while we explain.

If there is an empty void, there can be no life. But here we are looking at physicality. Don't forget that life started out in the non-physical realms or aspects and still does. Even what we consider to be 3D solidity is Astra illusion so there is no such thing as a solid universe (physicality).
Does this help us to solve the mystery of creation at all?
It certainly breaks a barrier because astral matter is easier to manipulate than physical matter.
But we need to find what came along to kickstart life.

We are going to say something that we hesitate to say because we cannot prove this.
It has always been assumed that God - who he is and where he came from - was deemed to be the ultimate mystery and we have said so ourselves although we knew that investigations were going on that were close to revealing a plausible concept for the creation of God.
Those conclusions have now been reached and we will present them to you although, as we said, we cannot prove the veracity of the theory.

It has been realised that we have been looking at the problem the wrong way round. We were looking through the wrong end of the telescope.

Our recent investigations and even more recent conclusions have revealed that life can only exist when personality exists and, in fact, the origin of life is personality.
Not your personality, not ours but the global concept of personality.

This is a new revelation and is why we are giving you this book at this time although it does just happened to fit nicely in the sequence of books we are giving you.

To return to personality.
We imagine that to have personality one would need to have a body and be 'alive' and that is how things are usually imagined, personality included, but we have recently realised that personality can exist outside of space/time and outside of life as we imagine it.
We have said, and we imagine this to be true, although we have no proof, that before there was God there was nothing. Just an empty void.

But we have realised that there is no such thing as nothing because nothing, by its very nature, has personality.
So, although we cannot see nothing, cannot measure or count it, the word nothing exists and that gives it meaning and meaning implies personality.
We do agree that this might sound as if we are clutching at straws but we hope that you might accept that some of our finest minds have worked conscientiously on this subject for a long time before coming up with this simple solution which we all believe to be true.

Obviously, we will do our best to explain this strange and somewhat outrageous statement that personality is the source of all life in our galaxy and, by extension, all galaxies no matter where they are to be found.

We have delved into personalities to a fair depth in this book but, so far, have always assumed that life existed and we have traced how personalities were linked to DNA and, ultimately, to the God spirit itself.

So, our job now is to go beyond when anything existed and follow the path that ended with creation. We go back to the time when, it is assumed, nothing existed.

As we have said, nothing can be produced from nothing but, once something exists it can be expanded upon almost without limit, which is what has happened in our galaxy and all the other galaxies and life forms that now exist.
We confidently expect that life will expand far into the future also, but that is not our concern.
Our concern is how life was created before creation!

We have mentioned that personality is the force responsible for this wonderful creation.
So, let us try to explain the type of personality that could have existed before creation.

Personality is connected to consciousness but the type of personality we wish to describe preceded consciousness.

In this long-ago time when, so we are told, there was nothing, as we said there had to be something to fire the starting pistol, so to speak.
This something was and is a form of consciousness that we have managed to link to personality which leads to life.
We must explain further to convince you.

It has always been assumed that before there was something there was nothing and this nothing has been described as no planets, no air, no lack of air, no life forces, no … anything!
This we accept.
Difficult as it is to visualise somewhere where nothing exists we can imagine it because those lucky enough to have been taken to where the Higher Self exists and, by extension, our God, will know that God exists in this nowhere place and will have had the strange experience of talking to their Higher Self whilst in this nowhere place.
So, we know that this nowhere place exists and we must try to explain how life came to exist in this nowhere place that, in turn, over vast eons of time created all that now exists in all dimensions.

This is where we need to expand our minds and take a leap of faith.

This nothingness, this nowhere place could not exist quite in that meaningless fashion.

To have nothing can be looked at another way and can be calculated as a lack of something.
But, by the very act of having nothing gives meaning to the word. And so to have nothing is, in itself, a positive force.
This is difficult to explain but let us give a childish example.
Suppose we assembled one hundred people and ask them to break into two groups, those who had money on them and those that did not.
Most would have some money about their person but, in these days of the use of credit cards, there are people who might have no money on them.
So, we break the group of people into two groups, those with money and those without.

Now, the group without money still have a presence. The fact that they have no money is sufficient to be able to identify them and they exist as a real group.
So, we hypothesize and present for your consideration that to have nothing does not mean quite what it suggests.
Nothing can be an identifiable force in its own right.

Now, the people who have been investigating this conundrum for long years are not foolish people and have considered this concept from every angle.
The scientific rule is that something can only be accepted as true if it is true in all cases.

The best minds available in heaven, including some well-known scientists and also angelic beings gathered together to examine this concept and have come to the conclusion that nothing is, in fact, a something force and, although nothing may apply to anything physical and, indeed, most things non-physical, there exists, nevertheless, by the very nature of nothingness a form of meaning that we term personality.

This is difficult to accept and we don't expect all people to be in agreement with this analysis.

So, can we explain this form of personality that is so different from the traditional meaning?
This personality implies that 'nothing', in the sense we give to it, is to say that this lack of anything has a deep intelligence.
It might well be the opposite of traditional intelligence but, for those who have been able to link with and to explore the area before there was anything, were impressed by just how concentrated how focused this nothingness was and is.
It became clear that this nothing this was as dynamic a force as any life could be - more so in many cases. Nothingness does not really exist. It is just an alternative force that had been, until that point, unknown.

So the wise beings that explored the area before life as we now know it, became more and more convinced that this area had its own form of creation, of personality.
So, over a long period of time, the finest minds explored the concept and were drawn to the inevitable conclusion that nothing exists in its own right and has meaning. It has personality.

Of course, one could argue that if nothing has meaning then who created nothing?
But search as we might we can find nothing that existed before 'nothing', if you follow our trend of thought.

But it does give us a breathing space and allows us to accept that life was able to develop from the concept of nothing and so we cling onto that concept for the moment.

We repeat, the latest wisdom suggests that before creation there was nothing but nothing is a real force and has personality.
From this strange nothingness, life was able to develop.
This is as far as we have got in our investigations and these revelations are very recent.
We in the Heavenly spheres can accept the idea of nothing being a real, live force.
Perhaps not alive in any sense that we could identify with but most of us in the Great White Brotherhood and beyond have expanded vision and thus are, perhaps, more able to accept concepts that many others would stumble at.

We do accept that it is easier to say that if nothing exists then nothing exists!
But, if you think about it, to say that nothing exists is to give existence to nothing.
Nothing becomes something.

But we must say that out investigations never cease and if, at some time in the future, we find another convincing meaning to how life started we will amend our conviction. We are never blocked behind any theory.

So we present this idea to you, which we believe to be true, and leave you to accept or reject the concept.
Assuming what has been concluded is true it gives the notion that personality is of paramount importance and existed before creation.

CHAPTER 17

THE END AND THE BEGINNING

We don't know what you made of that last chapter where we tried to justify the very strange and very unlikely concept that nothingness was, in fact, not only something but such an important something that it could create the foundation of all that now exists.

This leaves us in a quandary because, on the one hand, we feel somewhat obliged to try to expand in order to help you understand this strange concept and, on the other, to leave it as it is in the sure knowledge that time will help make things clear.

We should, perhaps, say that even we feel a little uneasy with the concept that nothing is something.

Most of us accept it as a working hypothesis and, as we have confidence in the brilliant minds that managed to discover this idea, we do not question the conclusions and, further, if it is true that there is really no such thing as nothing, it does help us formulate a foundation for life to commence.
But we do appreciate that for the majority of the world's population, especially those who are stuck in physicality, it runs against all logic. For many people either something exists or it does not.

We understand that point of view and we would not argue against it but, at the same time, there are huge numbers of people who proudly state if they cannot see, measure and quantify something it doesn't exist.
We have mentioned this before and have described some of the many things that we cannot see but that do exist: electricity for example. We can see and measure the effects but we cannot actually see electricity. Gravity is another. Life yet another. Wind yet another.

Looking at life from that point of view, if we can start to accept that things can exist without them being visible or measurable perhaps, eventually, it may be accepted that lack of anything is just another way of life presenting its facets to us.

But we do not wish to be accused of overkill. To quote Shakespeare. In Hamlet, Queen Gertrude says," The lady doth protest too much, methinks."
So we will stop here and turn to how, from that humble beginning of nothing being a positive force we called personality, it started to grow into the concepts of Gods.

Perhaps we should explain why the fact that nothing is a great deal and should be linked to personality because this does not seem at all likely at first glance.

So, we have this strange notion that before there was something, indeed, all that we now puzzle about, there was nothing but we hypothesize that nothing is something. We feel that we must make some effort to expand on this idea although, as we said, people in the future will be able to make the link more effectively than today's humans.

It would appear that there has never been truly 'nothing'. It is just that the system that we now know did not exist and so we assumed that before what we now understand to constitute life did not exist therefore there was nothing.
But it seems that there was something and this something we call personality.
So, we now believe that there has always been a force, a sort of life, although we could not link it to life as we now understand it to be.

This almost feels as if we are cheating in that we are just pushing back creation further and further into the past.
And yet we reach the point where any form of life as any of us understand it ceases to be but, it now appears that before our understanding of life there was a global force that was completely different to any life that we now have.

This life force was a composite whole and could not be divided up into different parts as we are able to do once the idea of God and galaxies came into being.

Thus, to understand the difference we have to trace life in the sense that we have described in our various books and lectures back to the point that it no longer exists and replace it with a sort of block of a totally different meaning.

We ask you to imagine if you can a personality block that has a form of life but nothing that could relate to life as we know it.

The strange thing is that this personality was and is totally unconnected to any form of life as we now know it to be and yet we are fairly sure that this original personality block was able, in some way, to open the door to the creation of all that now exists.
So there must be a connection.
If there is a connection we should be able to link this original personality block to the creative force that we call the creator God.

Therefore, we try to imagine this one, all connected block of personality, and allow time to modify it until it morphs into the creator God.
Then, from that, all the rest of the Jigsaw came to be.

But it started with a personality block.
We have a deep intuitive feeling that this personality block that existed in the past is identical to the personality block that will sound the death knell when our sense of creation ends.
In other words, life will continue for long ages until, one day, life comes together and forms one block of personality at which point it will create a creator God and it will all start again.

If this is true it implies that our disparate personalities will gradually join to become one whole personality and that will signal the end of one cycle of the wheel of life and life will join to the point where it left off and will restart to another cycle, another rotation of the wheel of life.

Of course, it really doesn't help much because it still does not say much about where life came from in the first place.
Nor does it tell us anything about the nature of the force that created life.

We know that life is vibration and that is really all we can say.

We understand that the next round of life is created from the personality block that ended the last cycle but we still have no idea of when and how it all started in the first place.

But what we are fairly sure about is that personality is the force that comes together until all of life becomes one block of personality.
Then life, whatever life is, decides that is has done enough and stops until it can create another creator God and life starts all over again.

We will state that new life starts the moment the old life ends. There is no break. That is why we can compare life to a wheel, endlessly turning.

We are of the opinion that the personality block, as it disappears, provides the motive force to promote the next turning of the wheel.
This implies that, as life comes together to create one personality, at the moment when the last life form gives up its individuality and joins the global personality then it all disappears releasing a vast amount of spiritual power and that is used to give the next wheel of life its spin.

So, once it started, it all works automatically, all the various life forms progressing towards perfection and, more importantly, gradually giving up its sense of individuality, its ego and joining together with all like-minded life forces to create this global personality.

This raises another point that we should explain.

We have stated in previous works that the God force - the ID - is constantly pushing us to survive at all costs and at the expense of other life forces if necessary.
We see this with plants that spread their leaves to get all the light they need and spread their roots to get all the nutrients they need.
Animals do much the same.
It is survival at all costs that is important.
But survival is a selfish act. Caring only for self at the expense of others.
This is what psychopaths do.
But, at the same time, this only applies to physicality and physicality is only a drop in the ocean of life.

Therefore, in order to reach the point where all life joins together to think as one would imply that physical life as we know It could not exist. Physical life requires one to survive at all costs but the personality required for life to reach its end implies all sense of individuality disappearing and all entities joining as one thought.

We have to imagine a life where physicality has no meaning and even the love force that motivates our galaxy being modified to incorporate a sort of pure energy with no particular emotion.

So, can we imagine, far into our future, a state where there is no physical life and all life forms, whatever they might be or whatever dimension they might live in are in a state that is outside of any emotions?
Can we imagine all life as one emotionless force that just exists?

Then what about the galaxy orbs we mentioned?
All the various Gods in charge of these galaxies?
The creator God itself?
What happens to all of these Gods?
We can only speculate but if it is true that all life must reach a point of just pure emotion and personality, pure energy if you will, we imagine that these Gods must also lose all sense of individuality and join with the rest of everything.

Now, our relation to any God has always been difficult to comprehend.

We imagine that our God, for instance, being the creator of all that exists - and here we are linking the directors of life and any other archangels to be included in the word God - has access to all the personalities although we explained that our God's theme was love. So it would seem that our God, if he has a personality like us, would be consumed with the desire to explore and create love in all its facets.
For those who have difficulty in understanding what we mean by this we must say that to understand what love truly is we must explore also hate because it is only possible to understand the subject if we also understands its opposite - hate.
Therefore, hate must exist as an anvil on which to strike with the hammer of love. We could describe this in the opposite manner also.
The hammer of hate striking the anvil of love.
Either way we need to two forces, love and hate.
This is how love is truly understood.

But we must assume that our God along with all the other Gods we mentioned must, at some point, give up their creative power and join with the rest of us in being this formless personality.
Lastly, we must also assume that the original creator God relinquishes its power also.
Then, at some point everything ceases to be and starts again with, we assume, a creator God being instantly formed from the power released from the demise of the old system.

Perhaps this is where the concept of the Phoenix bird rising from the ashes of its previous incarnation comes from.

Having tried, to a small extent, to explain and justify this strange concept, it all seems abstract as if it only concerns other life forms and not us but we would be wrong.

We are very much a part of these life forms and so, at some point far into the future we will discard our personalities and, eventually, disappear as all life disappears.

We know that there are people who have little understanding of life and will start to be uneasy thinking that this event will happen soon. We wish to reassure such people that, although we are fairly certain of what we are explaining and sure that these events will happen, we will say that it will occur far in the future.
Could we put a timescale on it? The answer is no but we would guess that we are talking about billions of years in our future so there is no need to panic.
All of us will continue our lives as they are now for long years into the future.
We hope this reassures you.

For the moment we are moving into the positive phase of the pendulum swing of creation.
This will last a long time.
Also, the population of Earth is steadily growing as an ever-increasing number of spirits volunteer to incarnate to take part in the ascension process.

We mentioned that, one day, far into the future, physical incarnation will cease and all life, animal, vegetable, mineral and human will cease to be.
So, one day there will be nothing physical and all life will remain in spiritual form. This will happen but is so far down the road of life that we cannot even imagine that it will happen.

But all things follow the same path: birth, growth, decline and death. The whole of our system must follow the same path. It is just the timescale that alters.
Our physical system came into being many billions of years ago and will continue for many billions of years before, finally, ceasing to be and life will start again somewhere.

Can you imagine people in billions of years asking the same questions that we now ask? Puzzling where we all came from and where we are going?

Apparently, this has happened countless times and will continue forever exactly as it is happening now … over and over again.

Life is, indeed, strange and is difficult to understand.

The strangest thing of all is that it can all be traced to personality and personality is linked to DNA.
We wonder what DNA can tell us about life?

That will be the next chapter of this book.

CHAPTER 18

PERSONALITY AND NEW LIFE

This chapter will carry on from the point that the last one finished which is to study how, as personality altered as life came to its end, so the DNA must have altered and, once life started again, how and if DNA was recreated.
Need we repeat that we are not talking about physical DNA as that will stop as physical incarnation stops so we will be considering the other sort of DNA, so-called junk DNA, which plays such an important role in the creation of personality and, indeed, most aspects of non-physical life as we have explained at great length in this and other works.

We have stated that DNA is heavily involved with the creation of personality and thus DNA is involved with most of the aspects of life whether it be mineral, vegetable, animal or human. Particularly human.

But we have, in the last chapter, explained that life reaches a point where it gives up all desire for individual personality and creates a global personality totally unlike any form of personality previously known.
This may be difficult to understand and so we will expand somewhat.

If you have followed our other teachings you will be aware that all life, particularly human, develops personalities and these personalities can be linked to the signs of the zodiac.
Therefore, our galaxy is home to all sentient life and each sentient being has a particular personality trend mixed with sub personalities.
But, at the same time, the theme of our galaxy is love.
So we have this rather strange mixture, totally unique to our galaxy, of sentient beings with widely different personalities living in a world the God of which promotes love.
Perhaps we should also say for those who do not know, if a person desires to have a physical incarnation he comes to planet Earth.
There are sound reasons why this is so and we have explained why before but let us just say that it was easier for God's archangels - the directors of life - to keep control of events by having them all together on one planet.
There are no other planets in our solar system with physical life on the surface, nor under the surface for that matter. All physical life incarnates exclusively on planet Earth.
The only life forms that incarnate elsewhere are minerals that combine to create other planets and moons but minerals are not really alive in the same degree that humans are.
People who create stories concerning life on the moon and on Mars, for instance, are either mistaken or they are describing reptilians and/or robots sent there for various reasons.
There are no actual people indigenous to the moon or Mars nor any other body for that matter. It is all contained on Earth.
Thus it is easier to control.

However, all life is one and when that far off day arrives that life decides to stop, all of existence, physical and spiritual, will disappear and that energy is used to recreate another turn of the wheel of life.
As far as we can see, once all life ceases, there is no other external God which creates the new life.
It is created by the massive amount of energy released by the disappearance of the old life.
It would appear that this cycle continues endlessly and because life is a spiritual force the energy released is exactly the same as was used to create the old life.
We feel that there might be even more energy released through the endeavours of life improving in spirituality but that is pure speculation on our part.
What we are sure of is that sufficient energy is released to create a new life, a new rotation of the wheel of life.

For those wondering how life can store energy and release it a bit at a time over billions of years, we remind you that time is an illusion and so, as one life disappears, the new life is created and actually lasts for a flash of time before disappearing again. It is how we regard time that gives the impression of countless years.

It is, of course, quite impossible for us to imagine that life, as far as we are all concerned, lasts for just a tiny moment before repeating the cycle but that is because we are conditioned to think of time as a linear force stretching from the past into the future.
But it is of no importance to worry about that.
Life is complicated enough without us trying to imagine life being created, destroyed and recreated billions of times a second.
Let us content ourselves to accepting life as we perceive it to be, a long slow linear progression.
But let us return to what happens to our DNA as our personalities are given up in favour of a collective one, no doubt totally different from any we can imagine.

So, we have, stored in the akashic record, a vast number of different personality types but none of these fit into the pattern required for this one, unique personality that must come together to prepare us all to disappear for the next cycle to commence.
And yet, this unique personality must exist somewhere or it could not be used.
So where is it?
To find it we must realise a number of things.

First, we would like to remind you that, one by one, as we reach perfection we dissolve into the Godhead and become one with God.
This, of course, is part of the circle of life - the wheel of life, if you wish.
So the day arrives when all living things; mineral, animal, flora and human cease to exist as independent objects and become one with God and assume God's personality, which is pure love.

We remind you that all was created by God - and we include his archangels, as usual - so even dimensions one and two and the lower fourth (all that can be connected to non-love) disappears into the loving force which is God. It all returns to God. This is, of course, in preparation for the final step of everything disappearing.

Then God reaches out into the part of the auras/dimensions that we told you about that is reserved just for God.
And from that reserved part he reaches into the reserve of the akashic record and extracts from that restricted zone the special type of DNA that only God can use which is the formless type of personality.

Now, we do realise that there are a number of Gods so there has to be a similar process going on that allows all these Gods to create the same formless personality.

We must also admit that there is a certain amount of speculation connected to these statements but we are sufficiently sure of what we stayed to present them to you.
As we have said, if at any time in the future we find that something is not quite correct we will rectify the information.

So we wish you to accept if you will that the day will come when all that exists are the various Gods (and the creator God) and all the Gods vibrate to the one, unique and formless personality, which is actually DNA.

This is where we have to reach into deep speculation as we know that at some point everything disappears and the energy contained in the personality DNA provides the energy for the next spin of the wheel of life.
But we are not quite sure how all this happens.

We do know that all the Gods resolve into this DNA and we also know that there remains the creator God.

What we are not sure of is the step that transforms what is left of the old spin of the wheel of life into the new.
There are a couple of possibilities and both of them concern the master creator.

Either, at some point even the master creator is absorbed as the last God force and then, as that personality disappears, the energy released starts the next step of life and, somehow, a master creator appears or the master creator remains and takes control of the birth process and directs the energy liberated by this personality disappearing to create and control the next spin of the wheel of creation.
In other words, either a new master creator God is formed or the old one remains eternally.

We have no knowledge of this event and thus cannot put any weight behind any theory.
It remains a mystery to us for the moment.

We hope you can appreciate that we are trying to delve billions of years into the future to the point where the wheel of life ends and a new one begins or we try to look back

billions of years into the past to the point that the last spin stopped and the one we now find ourselves in started.
Either way, we hope that you can appreciate that it is not a simple task to puzzle out what happened.

Modern day science delves ever further back in the past to try to discover the moment of creation but we are trying to look past that point to the moment of the last destruction.
If science, with all its resources, struggles we hope you will forgive us if we, too, struggle.
What we are sure of is that the old wheel of life reaches a point where it disappears and then a new one starts at the point that the old one stopped.

We do not have all the facts as to how the exact process works but we do know some things and we have presented them to you.
It seems to us that what is important in all this are two things, intimately connected:
1. Personality, and
2. DNA.
We are of the opinion that all construction is governed by these two things and without them nothing would exist.

We are very impressed in the manner in which the directors of life and the various other angelic and archangelic beings cleverly invented this wide-ranging force we call DNA and linked the relevant portion of it to personality thus freeing personality to act in a global sense through the aegis of this wonderful DNA.
We also realise that in the book on DNA we gave you we merely gave you an overview of DNA, as a complete compendium of how DNA is connected and facilitates every portion of life would have been virtually impossible.

Personality, on its own, would be a rather limited force but by linking it into DNA which, itself, is linked to virtually every other aspect of creation has enabled personality to have far greater importance.

We have decided to end this chapter here and to add just one more final chapter to this book before moving onto new pastures.

CHAPTER 19

ALIEN PERSONALITIES

So what else should we tell you about personalities?
We could fill many pages with information because, as we hope you have understood, what we refer to as personality is a basic building block of life and without disparate and collective personalities - despite sometimes being given different names - there would be no life as we know it.

But there is no point at this time in giving you too much new information because we would need to open doors into areas of life that none of you would be aware of and thus would have difficulty in accepting.
We have other subjects yet to discuss so we do not wish to expand on personalities much more.

But we thought that in this last chapter as many of you are interested in alien life we would explore, to a certain extent, the personalities that aliens might have, assuming that they have personalities. It won't take long.

You may remember that we gave you a book about aliens and said that there were two types of true ETs; those in the lower fourth dimension and those that use spare or unused personality aspects of us humans.
We also mentioned cousins of us that live on or underground the earth (the Tall Whites for instance) that have flying craft and are sometimes confused with aliens.
They are not. All aliens are non-physical, dimensional or inter dimensional entities.

So let us commence with those you call the Grays.
As you should know by now, the little grey, bulbous headed creatures you are familiar with from countless books, films and sightings are just robots created from various demonic beings found in the lower fourth dimension.
We have mentioned these demonic beings to a certain degree in this book but we will do so again as there are a certain number of these creatures (not all) that are involved with the UFO program.
You will, we hope, excuse us if we repeat information given elsewhere for the sake of those who have not read all our books nor watched all the videos.

You should know that there are a variety of entities in the lower fourth dimension. They are all negative and they are all of various negative power according to the destructive tasks they were created to do.
Their prime function is to act in the opposite fashion to the angels of construction.
As all life in incarnation comes to its end, these demonic forces spring into action to lower the vibration of whatever is dying and, gradually, the silver cord breaks, the spirit of whatever it is; plant, animal or human goes off to its astral home and the demonic forces cause the object to break down into its constituent atoms.

Now, as we have said, there has to be a variety of demonic forces according to the tasks that they must achieve.
It does not take a very high-powered demon to breakdown the atoms of a blade of grass compared with the forces required to break down a complicated structure.

Thus, we might say that the various demons would have a varying degree of intelligence - IQ if you wish.
The basic djinn would have a limited intelligence and thus a rather basic personality, just sufficient to perform its task, whereas some of the much more powerful demons have a large degree of intelligence.
We remind you that all of these beings are negative and so their intelligence, or personality, is always concentrated on negativity, destruction.

We might break off here to explain how a demonic force in the lower fourth dimension knows that an object in the sixth dimension, which is considered physical, knows when an object is dying and can spring into action.
The answer is that, as all is one, there is a constant and permanent communication at all times with all things.

This means, if we might mention you, that at all times, as you grow, positive angelic forces are monitoring you and pouring positive energy into you to keep you alive and following your life plan.
Life follows four phases: birth, growth, decline and death.

So, for all things, including you and us, when we were in incarnation, positive angels poured positive energy into us in the form of vibrations up to a certain time. Then the positive power was gradually reduced to allow the decline part of the cycle of life to commence.
Eventually, by the law of mutual attraction, the positive angels withdraw and the negative ones move in to reduce the frequency of the person, animal or plant and that reaches a point where the spirit can no longer animate the entity and the silver cord - that all things have - breaks and whoever or whatever it is goes off to the higher 4th dimension while the angels of destruction move fully in and start the decomposition aspect of death. It is all quite automatic.

But, as these demonic entities are alive - just as alive as any creature or human is - they must have intelligence and a certain personality.
It should be obvious that a basic djinn would have a limited personality and a really powerful demon a much more advanced personality.

All the time the entities from the lower 4th just do their job, which is getting rid of dead things from the 6th dimension, there is no problem.
But, as we have also said, black magicians have learnt to harness their power to cause harm to others.

There is an aspect of the powerful demons that enters this chapter.

The highly intelligent demons have a lot of free time because they are not called into action to perform their duties very often. The majority of destruction is left to the low powered djinn.
So, some demons became bored and decided to explore life in physicality - the 6th dimension.

Now, as they are a non-physical force they are not able actually to appear in our physical realms because of the difference in frequency between their world and ours.
Physical life, even though it is illusion, is of a higher frequency than the lower 4th so even the greatest of demons finds it impossible to raise its frequency to our higher frequency.

Demons can lower their frequencies, which is what they do when they break down the constituent parts of a now dead object but they cannot raise frequencies. Only positive angels and life can do that.
So, they found it impossible to enter 3D life.

We have already explained this but we will repeat.
Long ago, when planet Earth was in the grips of the negative swing of the pendulum of creation, certain demons were able to influence certain highly advanced but negative humans and gave them the plans for constructing the UFOs and the little grey robots that we still see today.

Once that was done the demons could overshadow the robots, which were sufficiently intelligent to receive telepathic communication from the demons and thus the demons could interact with humanity and try to find a way of creating a human/demon (or alien) hybrid so as to gain a foothold on Earth.
This they failed to do. It is just as well.
Could you imagine people walking about with the personality of a powerful negative demon?
It would be bad enough but if ever they got into positions of power the effect would have been catastrophic.
Life is bad enough on Earth with the archon Influenced people who control the planet. However, as we have said, ascension will reduce the numbers and the powers of these people.

It is perhaps surprising to find that the alien life that we think we discovered interacting with us quite recently has, in fact, been happening for many hundreds (thousands) of years but it should not really be a surprise as even cave paintings often depict images of craft and/or beings clearly far different and far in advance to modern life. Certainly far different to life as seen by cavemen.

Now, what concerns and interests us is the personalities of these demonic entities.
We are not sure that we can analyse individual demons and discover their individual personalities but we can, at least, make some educated guesses.

For a start we are very familiar with the basic djinn and, if we may say, many of you should be familiar with them as they frequently make appearances in our daily lives. It is the fact that most people walk about with their eyes shut, if you will excuse us for insulting you somewhat, that enables them to operate in our world unseen.
In fact, basic djinn cannot really enter our 3D reality, as we have just said, but they can enter the etheric realm which is so close to physicality that many people can see into it and most digital photographic cameras can also capture djinn on both still and moving images.

Djinn are able to enter the etheric because they are so basic in nature that they are not really evil in the sense that highly developed demons are and thus their frequency is not far removed from the etheric realms.
People with even a basic ability to operate in psychic planes can see some djinn. However, most people have trained themselves to ignore any strange phenomena and so the djinn pass unnoticed.
Perhaps this is just as well as to interact with even the most basic of djinn, for an untrained person, would be unwise. Even the most basic of djinn is part of the negative forces so it would and could be dangerous for untrained people to interact with them. Those firmly on the side of good would want nothing to do with them, leaving only those interested in negativity to desire to interact with them.

But do djinn have individual personalities? We think not. We would consider them more to be like worker ants or bees, just doing their job.
However, this is not quite true as they have often been observed aping human or animal life, pretending to be something like a cat, a dog or some other life force. They try to imitate humans but the resulting shapes are not very convincing.
We notice that they do have curiosity and also fear quite developed so those are two aspects of personality. More than that is less obvious.

However, high powered demons are different indeed.
It is their advanced intelligence that has enabled them to have UFOs and robots constructed.

No demon can influence a good person due to the difference in frequency between them and good people.
But they can and do influence people who have negativity in their personalities.
So, this suggests to us that high powered demons have a developed but negative personality and have for a long time been able to overshadow negative people.
This is still going on, of course, in the underground bases where negative types of scientists of many disciplines work with the robots who are being controlled by demons. Therefore, we assume that, by the law of mutual attraction, if there are scientists, politicians and other rulers of the world, many of whom we consider to have negative personalities, the demons would have similar personalities.

We try to stay away from negative people but if and when we examine and analyse the personalities of various individuals involved with what we might call ET agendas or programs, we find people with very powerful, dominant personalities, often acting without hesitation to cause harm and even murder to those who either get in their way or need to be tortured or murdered to advance a program, we can imagine that demons would be very similar.

There are differences of course. Humans that cause harm to life, whatever that life is, when their incarnations end, find themselves in hell paying for their crimes whereas demons are immortal.
Another difference is that demons cannot directly operate in the 6th dimension where we are so they need to harness the energy of either the robots or the various humans with whom they work.
But the result is much the same.

If we examine the personalities of the humans who are involved with, either black magic or the so-called space program, including trying to produce hybrid humans, animals or trying to produce modified creatures - part human and part animal - we can easily understand the personalities that intelligent demons would have.
We advise anyone involved with these programs and that are dealing with demons that they are playing with fire.
A demon is a negative entity and exists to destroy. But, being intelligent, they are willing to work with scientists, politicians and any individual or groups on a seemingly positive program but one can be sure that the end result, if and when the end of the program arrives, will be negative and will cause destruction and unhappiness to as many as it is possible to involve.
Demons are negative and their personalities are negative.
It is a pity that so many people involved with these secret programs do not realise this, but being negative themselves, it is a question of birds of a feather flocking together.

Therefore, although it is not easy for us to fully understand the personalities of demons it appears to us that if we are aware of the personalities of those who work with them via the robots there must be a similarity.
You may have noticed yourself that it is very difficult to work with people who have personalities diametrically opposed to one's own, so by examining the personalities of those humans who do interact with demons we can get some idea of the personalities of demons.
There are a number of different groups of people involved with demons.
The first would be the military who have been promised advanced technology in exchange for helping the demon aliens.
We do not wish to insult anyone so if we use language that seems negative we hope both you and they will forgive us.
Military people have to be, by and large, rather special.
By that we mean that the security guards have to have personalities that do not question orders. They are told to patrol an area and keep it safe from any intrusion and that is what they do.
What their reaction is to any unusual life forces they come across or what their reaction is to any people or animals shut in cages would not be like ours.

We might well be horrified to see horrific scenes but the job of a security guard is just to make sure that no one from outside the complex penetrates and that nothing escapes.
Then, of course, we have the officer classes that would be involved with the demonic agenda.
We are sorry to say that the type of officer that would be attracted to helping develop programs might not be the sort of person of high intelligence.
Military circles and military folk tend to be the sort that accept, sometimes with pride, that they are part of an important and secret project and so they consider it an honour to ensure absolute secrecy and will go to great lengths to work with demonic alien forces, providing all the necessary facilities and materials to help these aliens.
The final agenda is not their problem only as far as their rank involves them with different levels of complexity.
Then we have the scientists that help the grey robots and, of course, their demonic masters.
Once again, those recruited to work on these projects have little regard for the suffering caused to people and animals, the results of their experiments. They put into action the desires of those higher up than them and justify what they do because they are pushing science forward.
Lastly, as regards our little discussion, we have a small number of politicians and/or secret service groups who are happy to help implement the whole agenda.

Now, from the above description, we can interpellate into the demonic mind and see that, according to the intelligence of various demons, there would be more or less the equivalent in the demonic group of the various human groups involved with the alien agenda.

Let us now consider the other type of aliens. Those that are created from unused personality bundles. For those who have no idea what we are describing please read the book on aliens we gave you.

This group, in principle, should have personalities not dissimilar to ours as they are, in fact, us.
So, we expect to find some with good, bad and indifferent personalities.
However, it has been our experience when dealing with this group of aliens that curiosity tends to be highly developed.
Thus, we find that this group also tend to be positive. It would be difficult to combine curiosity with negativity.
When we were describing somewhat negative military people we noticed that security guards, for example, had almost no curiosity. They obeyed orders without question.
One cannot be of that type if one has curiosity highly developed. So we generally find that curious people tend to be fairly positive.
We find this also with the groups of personality bundles that desire to become aliens.
They have curiosity, positivity and kindness developed .
They may or may not have spiritual awareness developed but one can be a good person without having spirituality developed.

Therefore, our description of this group - constituted from personality bundles - is short.

They tend to be curious first and foremost which is why they decide to become aliens and have the desire to explore the 6th dimension, which is where you are at the moment.
But they are also peaceful, loving entities and it is a pleasure to deal with them.

Thus we have two types of aliens.
1. The demonic forces that are entirely negative.
2. The personality bundles which tend to be the opposite. Kind, peaceful loving entities that wish us no harm and that will help us if they can.
This is not to say that all personality bundles are like that. It is those that decide to become aliens that tend to be nice.

So, we will end this chapter and this book here.
As is so often the case we have tried to explain personalities to you but have merely scratched the surface.

We hope that some of you at least have got something from this difficult subject.
We have done our best to explain it as simply as possible but it is a complex subject.
We will expand more in years to come.

Made in the USA
Columbia, SC
08 October 2020